Bibliografische Information der Deutschen Nationalbibliothek:

Die Deutsche Bibliothek verzeichnet diese Publikation in der Deutschen National-
bibliografie; detaillierte bibliografische Daten sind im Internet über http://dnb.d-
nb.de/ abrufbar.

Impressum:

Copyright © 2010 GRIN Verlag, Open Publishing GmbH
Druck und Bindung: Books on Demand GmbH, Norderstedt Germany
ISBN: 9783668367937

Dieses Buch bei GRIN:

http://www.grin.com/de/e-book/306900/die-benachteiligung-von-schuelern-mit-
migrationshintergrund-migration

Peter Dähn

Die Benachteiligung von Schülern mit Migrationshinter-grund. Migration in Deutschland

GRIN Verlag

GRIN - Your knowledge has value

Der GRIN Verlag publiziert seit 1998 wissenschaftliche Arbeiten von Studenten, Hochschullehrern und anderen Akademikern als eBook und gedrucktes Buch. Die Verlagswebsite www.grin.com ist die ideale Plattform zur Veröffentlichung von Hausarbeiten, Abschlussarbeiten, wissenschaftlichen Aufsätzen, Dissertationen und Fachbüchern.

Besuchen Sie uns im Internet:

http://www.grin.com/

http://www.facebook.com/grincom

http://www.twitter.com/grin_com

Inhaltsverzeichnis

I Einleitung 2

II Migration in Deutschland 3

II.1 Geschichte der Migration 3

II.2 Migration und Schule - Von der Ausländerpädagogik zum Integrationskonzept 4

II.3 Migrationshintergründe 6

II.3.1 Asylanten und Asylrecht, Flüchtlinge 7

II.3.2 Aussiedler und Spätaussiedler 8

II.3.3 Gastarbeiter 8

III. Literaturverzeichnis (inkl. weiterführender Literatur) 10

I Einleitung

Die Wanderungsbewegung von Menschen auf der ganzen Welt hat in den letzten 20 Jahren zugenommen und somit an Bedeutung für Politik, Wirtschaft und das Sozialwesen gewonnen. Allein zwischen 1990 und 2000 ist die Migration um etwa 46 Prozent angestiegen. Dieser Anstieg resultiert aus unterschiedlichen Gründen, wie beispielsweise dem Zusammenbruch der ehemaligen Sowjetunion und somit des gesamten Ostblocks. Ungünstige wirtschaftliche Veränderungen, schlechte soziale Bedingungen oder aber auch Kriege ließen die Menschen aus ihren Heimatländern fliehen, um in anderen Ländern ein besseres Leben führen zu können. Diese Menschen müssen im Aufnahmeland integriert werden, was durch Einbürgerung, soziale Sicherung oder auch mit dem Zugang zum Arbeitsmarkt geschehen kann.

In dieser Arbeit werde ich auf die Migration in Deutschland eingehen, dabei sollen Migrationshintergründe und die Geschichte der Migration knapp dargelegt werden.

Um den Lesefluss der Arbeit zu erleichtern, wird auf die feminine Geschlechtsform verzichtet und stattdessen lediglich die maskuline Form der Personenbezeichnung verwendet. Gemeint sind allerdings stets die weiblichen und männlichen Personen. Weiterhin sind, insofern von ausländischen Kindern, Jugendlichen oder Familien gesprochen wird, stets alle Gruppen mit Migrationshintergrund gemeint und somit auch jene, die bereits einen deutschen Pass und damit die deutsche Staatsangehörigkeit besitzen.

II Migration in Deutschland

II.1 Geschichte der Migration

Bereits 1871 spielte Zuwanderung ins Ruhrgebiet eine große Rolle, später im nationalsozialistischen Deutschland betrug der Anteil ausländischer Arbeiter, vor allem in der Kriegswirtschaft, 19,9%.[1] Nach dem Ende des II. Weltkrieges war das Land bevölkerungsmäßig stark geschwächt, wodurch sich ein Arbeitskräftemangel manifestierte, der auch in der Zeit des Wirtschaftswachstums noch akut war. Aufgrund dieses Umstandes kam es zu Verträgen zwischen Deutschland und verschiedenen süd- und außereuropäischen Staaten, bei denen es Ziel war, Arbeitskräfte für die Bundesrepublik zu gewinnen. Diese Personengruppe sollte spezifische Qualifikationen in ihrem jeweiligen Berufsfeld erhalten, um auch später den Industrien ihrer Heimatländer dienlich zu sein. Ursprünglich war dabei eine Aufenthaltsdauer von einem Jahr für die Gastarbeiter vorgesehen.[2] Da sich dieser Aufenthalt, durch den anhaltenden wirtschaftlichen Aufschwung, jedoch verlängerte, holten die Gastarbeiter ihre Familien nach, die von der Politik gewollten Billigarbeiter entwickelten sich langsam aber stetig zu Einwanderungsfamilien, denen es fern lag, Deutschland wieder zu verlassen. Allein für das Ruhrgebiet werden für 1955 etwa sechs Millionen Arbeitsmigranten gezählt.[3] Dabei war vor allem ein Nachzug von Kindern durch die Bundesregierung nicht geplant. Carolin Reißlandt unterteilt die Migrationsbewegung in folgende fünf Phasen: 1.Phase 1955 bis 1973: Anwerbung ausländischer Arbeitskräfte, In der zweiten Phase kam es infolge der einsetzenden Ölkrise zu einem Anwerbestopp für ausländische Arbeitskräfte und zur Konsolidierung der Ausländerbeschäftigung, die Anwerbeverträge seitens der Bundesregierung wurden gekündigt. Aufgrund der Krise waren die wirtschaftlichen Verhältnisse auch in den Heimatländern der Gastarbeiter desolat, so dass eine Rückkehr nicht von ökonomischem Nutzen für die Arbeiter war. Des Weiteren konnte es sich Deutschland nicht erlauben, einen Großteil von ihnen auszuweisen, da zwischenzeitlich viele Wirtschafts- und Dienstleistungszweige durch ausländische Werktätige überrepräsentiert waren. Während der 3.Phase von 1979 bis 1980 existierten konkurrierende Integrationskonzepte, bevor es in der 4.Phase zwischen 1981 und 1990 zu einer Wende in der Ausländerpolitik kam. Zwischen den Jahren 1991 und 1998, der fünften Phase, kam es immer wieder zu Dementi und

---

[1] Baethge, Martin (2005): Berichterstattung zur sozioökonomischen Entwicklung in Deutschland. Arbeit und Lebensweisen, Wiesbaden: Verlag für Sozialwissenschaften, S.351

[2] Seitz, Stefan (2006): Migrantenkinder und positive Schulleistungen, Bad Heilbrunn: Verlag Julius Klinkhardt , S.10

[3] Baethge (2005), S.351

3

abschließend zur praktischen Akzeptanz der Einwanderungssituation und letztlich in der sechsten Phase, in den Jahren 1998 bis 2004 zur Debatte über Staatsangehörigkeit und Zuwanderung. Hauptkern der Diskussion war im Verlauf dieser Jahre die Frage, ob Deutschland Einwanderungsland sei oder nicht.[4]

II.2 Migration und Schule - Von der Ausländerpädagogik zum Integrationskonzept

In den letzten 50 bis 60 Jahren sind Menschen aus den verschiedensten Regionen der Welt und mit unterschiedlichsten Beweggründen nach Deutschland eingewandert. Viele dieser Migranten holten im Verlauf der Jahre ihre Familien nach Deutschland, um sich hier auf Dauer niederzulassen, um vor allem einen besseren Lebensstandard zu genießen. Es versteht sich dabei von selbst, dass auch die Kinder der ausländischen Familien beschult werden müssen, um ihnen eine bestmögliche Ausbildung zu gewährleisten.[5] Dies wurde im Verlauf der Jahre unterschiedlich gehandhabt. Die Schulpflicht wird in Deutschland aufgrund der Kulturhoheit der Länder durch eben diese geregelt. Dabei gibt es teilweise unterschiedliche Direktiven zur Durchführung. Bereits auf der Kultusministerkonferenz vom 3.Dezember 1971 beschlossen die Minister, dass ausländische Kinder in die entsprechende Klasse ihres Geburtsjahres aufzunehmen seien, insofern sie der deutschen Sprache der jeweiligen Stufe entsprechend mächtig sind. Ebenfalls wurde die Möglichkeit in Erwägung gezogen, spezielle Vorbereitungsklassen einzurichten, um die Schüler auf ihre Jahrgangsstufe vorzubereiten. Insbesondere sollte auch die Muttersprache in den Unterricht mit einbezogen werden, sowie eine adäquate Schulung für Lehrkräfte erfolgen. Bei einer der nächsten Konferenzen 1976 bestätigte man erneut diese Beschlüsse und traf einige weitere Regelungen in Bezug auf den Unterricht für ausländische Schüler. Dabei wurde die Dauer der Vorbereitungsklassen auf maximal zwei Jahre festgelegt und gleichzeitig sollten weitere spezielle Fördermaßnahmen ermöglicht werden. Die Überweisung auf Sonderschulen, auf die ich später noch zu sprechen komme, sollte den gleichen gültigen Regelungen entsprechen, welche auch für die deutschen Schüler galten. Auf einer der letzten Kultusministerkonferenzen vom 25.Oktober 1996 wurden die Kriterien der Toleranz und Akzeptanz gegenüber ausländischen Mitbürgern in den

---

[4] Auf eine detaillierte Beschreibung der einzelnen Phasen soll an dieser Stelle verzichtet werden
hierzu Reißlandt, Carolin (2005): Migration in Ost- und Westdeutschland 1955 – 2004
URL: http://www.bpb.de/themen/8Q83M7,0,0,Migration_in_Ost_und_Westdeutschland
_von_1955_bis_2004.html, [Zugriff am 08.12.2009]
[5] An dieser Stelle soll nur eine kurze Ausführung über die Empfehlungen der Kultusministerkonferenzen erfolgen, auf eine ausführlichere Darstellung wird an dieser Stelle verzichtet. Weitere Ausführungen in Seitz (2006), S.15-30

4

Vordergrund gerückt. Die Minister waren sich einig, dass diese Eigenschaften oftmals vor allem durch erwachsene Vorbilder nicht „gelebt" werden und Kinder und Jugendliche somit diese Stereotype und Einstellungen häufig ohne Hinterfragen übernehmen. Man sah die Pädagogik in der Pflicht zu handeln, um Vorurteile abzubauen und eine Diskriminierung von ausländischen Schülern zu vermeiden bzw. zu verhindern. Am 24.Mai 2005 wurden auf der Kultusministerkonferenz die sprachlichen Probleme der Schüler mit Migrationshintergrund maßgeblich auf die familiären Umstände zurückgeführt. Dabei seien vor allem die sozialen Bedingungen, denen die Familie unterliegt, hauptsächlich ausschlaggebend für den schulischen Erfolg der Kinder. An dieser Stelle kam es zu Vorschlägen, das eine Einführung muttersprachlichen Unterrichts am Nachmittag möglich wäre, Deutsch als Zweitsprache in den Lehrplan aufzunehmen sei und vor allem, dass auch Kindern von Asylsuchenden die Schulpflicht zu ermöglichen sei. Da aber, wie bereits erwähnt, die Bildungshoheit bei den einzelnen Bundesländern liegt, ist die Umsetzung der Beschlüsse der Kultusministerkonferenz ein besonderes Problem. Die Ergebnisse der Konferenz haben somit lediglich empfehlenden Charakter.

Gerade in den Anfangsjahren der Gastarbeiteranwerbung in Deutschland und später bei Einreisewellen von Flüchtlingen und Asylbewerbern stellte sich immer wieder die Frage, ob die mit- oder nachgereisten Kinder der Arbeiter zu beschulen seien, oder nicht. Die Entscheidung fiel letztlich zu Gunsten der Kinder, dass diese den deutschen Schülern rechtlich gleichzustellen seien und der Schulpflicht unterliegen. Ein Grund für diese politische Entscheidung ist darin zu suchen, dass Folgekosten in Form von Sozialhilfe oder auch Unterstützung der Kinder durch Sozialarbeit höher liegen würden, als sie der allgemeinen Schulpflicht zuzuführen. Des Weiteren wurde auch von der Idee Abstand genommen, separate Schulen ausschließlich für Kinder mit Migrationshintergrund einzurichten, stattdessen ging man zur Idee des Integrationskonzeptes über.[6]

Das Konsortium Bildungsberichterstattung hat in seinem Bericht über Bildung in Deutschland von 2006 folgendes festgestellt.

„Es besteht Einvernehmen in Politik und Wissenschaft, dass dem Erziehungs-, Bildungs- und Qualifikationssystem eine Schlüsselfunktion für den langfristigen Erfolg der gesellschaftlichen Integration von Migranten(kindern) zukommt. Besonders angesichts der demographischen Entwicklung sind Förderung und (Aus-)Bildung junger Migrantinnen und Migranten – als

---

[6] Gomolla, Mechthild & Radtke, Frank-Olaf (2007): *Institutionelle Diskriminierung. Die Herstellung ethnischer Differenz in der Schule*, 2.Auflage, Wiesbaden: VS Verlag für Sozialwissenschaften, S.83f

Kinder der einzig wachsenden Bevölkerungsgruppe – für gesellschaftliche Produktivität und gesellschaftlichen Wohlstand von großer Bedeutung."[7]

Aus diesem Zitat geht hervor, dass aufgrund sinkender Nachwuchszahlen bei deutschen Familien ein besonderes Augenmerk auf die Familien mit Migrationshintergrund und dabei besonders auf deren Kinder gelegt werden muss. Das Konsortium betrachtet Zuwanderung zu einem als Aufgabe und Chance, schließt aber auch aus, das einzig die Bildungsinstitutionen zu einer gelungenen Integration ausländischer Kinder beitragen können. Vielmehr erachten sie es als nötig, dass die Politik, sowie das soziale und ökonomische Umfeld Hilfestellungen leisten müssen. Das Hauptziel, welches erreicht werden soll, ist, dass die Schüler durch Bildung besser integriert werden, um letztlich ihrem deutsch Pendant in Abschlüssen und Kompetenzen in nichts mehr nachzustehen. Auch wenn sich im Laufe der letzten Jahre gute Entwicklungen im Bereich der schulischen Bildung auf Seiten der Schüler mit Migrationshintergrund zeigen, so haben internationale, sowie nationale Schulleistungstests doch offengelegt, dass sich starke Diskrepanzen bei den erreichten Schulabschlüssen gegenüber ihrem deutschen Pendant zeigen. Hierbei fällt besonders auf, dass ausländische Schüler am Gymnasium deutlich unterrepräsentiert sind, jedoch auf der Hauptschule einen großen Anteil der Schülerschaft ausmachen.[8]

II.3 Migrationshintergründe

Das mit Migration Menschen verschiedenster Herkunft und aus unterschiedlichsten Gründen ihren Weg nach Deutschland gesucht haben, ergibt sich aus den bisher erfolgten Ausführungen. Auch bei den Kindern und Jugendlichen muss im Sinne eines Migrationskonzeptes beachtet werden, ob diese als selbst zugewanderte Personen nach Deutschland kamen, oder ob sie hier geboren sind, und somit der Kategorie der zweiten Generation zugeordnet werden.

In Deutschland wurden bis zum Jahr 2005 statistische Erfassungen der Menschen mit Migrationshintergrund nach dem Ausländerkonzept vorgenommen, ein Wechsel zum Migrationskonzept erfolgte hier durch den Mikrozensus. Dieser wurde nötig, da seit dem

---

[7] Konsortium Bildungsberichterstattung (2006): *Bildung in Deutschland. Ein indikatorengestützter Bericht mit einer Analyse zu Bildung und Migration,* Bielefeld : W. Bertelsmann Verlag GmbH & Co. KG, S.137
[8] Konsortium Bildungsberichterstattung (2006), S.137

1.Januar 2000 für in Deutschland geborene Kinder ausländischer Eltern eine Gesetzesnovelle gilt.[9] Diese besagt:

„...(3) Durch die Geburt im Inland erwirbt ein Kind ausländischer Eltern die deutsche Staatsangehörigkeit, wenn ein Elternteil

1. seit acht Jahren rechtmäßig seinen gewöhnlichen Aufenthalt im Inland hat und...“[10]

Durch diese statistischen Erhebungen können seitdem spezielle Daten zum Migrationshintergrund aufgeschlüsselt werden, was mit dem bisherigen Konzept so nicht möglich gewesen ist. Besonders für die Auswertung dieser Daten, auch im Hinblick auf bildungspolitische Fragestellungen, ergeben sich nunmehr realitätsnähere Chancen.[11] In Deutschland haben derzeit etwa 15,4 Millionen Menschen einen Migrationshintergrund.[12] Für das Bildungssystem ist dabei jedoch nur der Personenkreis der unter 25-Jährigen relevant. Die Herkunft der Kinder ist dabei äußerst heterogen. Ein beträchtlicher Teil von ihnen kommt aus der Türkei, aber ebenso aus den ehemaligen Anwerbestaaten und aus der ehemaligen Sowjetunion. Dabei sind natürlich nicht alle Schüler der Gruppe der Selbstzugewanderten zuzuordnen, sondern besonders aus der Gruppe der türkischen Kinder sind viele bereits in Deutschland geboren und gehören somit der zweiten oder gar dritten Generation der Kinder mit Migrationshintergrund an.[13]

II.3.1 Asylanten und Asylrecht, Flüchtlinge

In Deutschland genießen politisch verfolgte Menschen Asylrecht.[14] Inzwischen sind es allerdings nicht nur politische Umstände, die die Menschen zu einer Flucht aus ihrem Heimatland veranlassen. Aufgrund von kriegerischen Auseinandersetzungen, ökologischen aber auch ökonomischen Faktoren nehmen die Flüchtlingsströme zu. Diesen Strömungen versucht man durch Gesetze entgegenzuwirken.[15] Die sozialen Möglichkeiten für die Gruppe der Asylanten sind in Deutschland aufgrund der ihnen auferlegten Rechtsstatuten sehr gering.

---

[9] ebenda, S.139
[10] §4 Staatsangehörigkeitsgesetz (StAG), URL: http://www.gesetze-im-internet.de/rustag/__4.html [Zugriff am 12.01.2009]
[11] speziell zur Aufschlüsselung der Statistischen Erhebung des Mikrozensus und zur Heterogenität der Migration Konsortium Bildungsberichterstattung (2006), S.139
[12] Statistische Ämter des Bundes und der Länder (2009): *Bevölkerung nach Migrationsstatus regional. Ergebnisse des Mikrozensus 2007*, Wiesbaden : Hessisches Statistisches Landesamt, S.12
[13] Konsortium Bildungsberichterstattung (2006), S.140ff
[14] Zum Asylrecht Deutschlands Art.16a Grundgesetz (2001), S.19
[15] Seitz (2006), S.11f

Im Falle einer Eingliederung nach langer Aufenthaltsdauer führt dieser Umstand zu einer sehr schwachen sozialen Eingliederung.[16]

II.3.2 Aussiedler und Spätaussiedler

Die Zuwanderung von Aussiedlern bzw. Spätaussiedlern begann in der Phase nach dem II. Weltkrieg und setzt sich noch bis in die heutige Zeit hinein fort. Diese Personengruppe zählt gemäß Artikel 116 des Deutschen Grundgesetzes nicht zu den Ausländern.[17] 1993 kam es zum Erlass des Kriegsfolgenreinigungsgesetzes, was zu einem sprunghaften Anstieg des Zuzuges von der nun als Spätaussiedler bezeichneten Gruppe führte. Gleichzeitig war auch die Auflösung der Warschauer-Pakt-Staaten mit verantwortlich für den Ansturm seitens der Spätaussiedler.[18] Problematisch ist für empirische Untersuchungen zur Bildungsbeteiligung von Schülern mit Migrationshintergrund, dass diese Personengruppe erst seit 1990 durch die Integrationspolitik erfasst wird. Bis dahin verlief die Integration eher stillschweigend neben der von Gastarbeitern und Asylsuchenden. Durch die Veränderungen in den Gesetzen zur Zuwanderung von Aussiedlern wurden die sozialen Zustände der Aussiedler drastisch verschlimmert.

II.3.3 Gastarbeiter

Aufgrund der Nachkriegssituation in Deutschland, sowie dem damit resultierenden Problem des Arbeitskräftemangels während der Expansion der Weltwirtschaft, kam es zu Verträgen zwischen Deutschland und verschiedenen südeuropäischen, aber auch außereuropäischen Staaten. Ziel hierbei war es, Arbeitskräfte für die Bundesrepublik zu gewinnen, ihnen spezifische Qualifikationen zukommen zu lassen, damit sie später der Industrie in ihren Heimatländern dienlich werden konnten.[19] Ursprünglich war dabei eine Aufenthaltsdauer von einem Jahr vorgesehen. Da diese Aufenthaltsspanne jedoch verlängert wurde, holten die Gastarbeiter ihre Familien nach Deutschland nach, die von der Politik gewollten „Billigarbeiter" entwickelten sich langsam aber stetig zu Einwanderungsfamilien, denen es fern lag Deutschland wieder zu verlassen. Aus diesem Grund erhöhte sich der

---

[16] Sachverständigenrat für Zuwanderung und Integration (2004): *Migration und Integration. Erfahrungen nutzen, Neues wagen (Jahresgutachten 2004)*, Berlin: ohne Verlag, S.12f
[17] Art.116, Grundgesetz (2001), S.59
[18] Sachverständigenrat für Zuwanderung und Integration (2004), S.99ff
[19] Seitz (2006), S.10

Familiennachzug stetig. Vor allem ein Nachzug von Kindern war durch die Bundesregierung nicht geplant.[20] Durch die Ölkrise 1973 kündigte man seitens der Bundesregierung die Anwerbeverträge. In der Zwischenzeit waren aber auch die wirtschaftlichen Verhältnisse in den Ländern der Gastarbeiter desolat und Deutschland konnte es sich ebenso nicht erlauben, einen Großteil von ihnen auszuweisen, da viele Wirtschaftszweige, vor allem im Niedriglohnsektor, mit ausländischen Arbeitskräften überrepräsentiert waren.

Man könnte an dieser Stelle weitere Ausführungen zur Kategorisierung von Migrationshintergründen machen, bzw. die einzelnen Gruppen mit ihren Wanderungshintergründen näher betrachten, da dazu aber schon zahlreiche Werke erschienen sind, soll an dieser Stelle auf eine tiefgründige Aufarbeitung verzichtet werden.[21]

---

[20] Emmerich, Michaela (1987): *Die soziale Situation ausländischer Kinder in der Bundesrepublik Deutschland.* in Buchkremer, Hansjosef & Emmerich, Michaela (Hrsg.)(1987): *Ausländerkinder. Sonderpädagogische Fragestellungen.* Hamburg: EB-Verlag, S.54f
[21] Literatur zum Thema Migration u.a. Angenendt, Steffen (1997): *Migration und Fluch.: Aufgaben und Strategien für Deutschland, Europa und die internationale Gemeinschaft.* Bonn: Bundeszentrale für Polit. Bildung. (Schriftenreihe / Bundeszentrale für Politische Bildung, 342)

III. Literaturverzeichnis (inkl. weiterführender Literatur)

Abels, Heinz (2007): *Einführung in die Soziologie. Band 1: Der Blick auf die Gesellschaft.* 3. Auflage. Wiesbaden : Verlag für Sozialwissenschaften

Apitzsch, Giesela (1998): *Situationsbericht zu Sonderschulen. Fakten und Daten.* in: Kommunale Ausländerinnen- und Ausländervertretung (KAV) der Stadt Frankfurt am Main (Hrsg.) (1998): *Sonderschulen. Schulen für Migrantenkinder? Hintergründe einer Problematik. Möglichkeiten der Prävention. Dokumentation einer Anhörung am 21.November 1996,* Mönchengladbach: Forum Verlag Godesberg GmbH, S.15-21

Autorengruppe Bildungsberichterstattung (2008): *Bildung in Deutschland 2008. Ein indikatorengestützter Bericht mit einer Analyse zu Übergängen im Anschluss an den Sekundarbereich I,* Bielefeld : W. Bertelsmann Verlag GmbH & Co. KG

Baethge, Martin (2005): *Berichterstattung zur sozioökonomischen Entwicklung in Deutschland. Arbeit und Lebensweisen,* Wiesbaden: Verlag für Sozialwissenschaften

Bednarz-Braun, Iris & Heß-Meining, Ulrike (2004): *Migration, Ethnie und Geschlecht: Theorieansätze, Forschungsstand, Forschungsperspektiven.* Wiesbaden: VS Verlag für Sozialwissenschaften

Behr, Vera (1986): *Türkische Kinder und Jugendliche in deutschen Schulen. Kulturelle Hintergründe.* In: Tumat, Alfred J. (1986): *Interkulturelle Erziehung in Praxis und Theorie. Band 3. Migration und Integration. Ein Reader.* Sulzberg/Allgäu : Pädagogischer Verlag Burgbücherei Schneider, S.152-167

Böhm, Winfried (2005): *Wörterbuch der Pädagogik.* 16.Auflage, Stuttgart: Alfred Kröner Verlag

Bohn, Cornelia & Hahn, Alois (1999): *Pierre Bourdieu.* in: Kaesler, Dirk (Hrsg.)(1999): *Klassiker der Soziologie. Band II. Von Talcott Parsons bis Pierre Bourdieu.* München: C.H.Beck, S.252-271

Diefenbach, Heike (2008): *Kinder und Jugendliche aus Migrantenfamilien im deutschen Bildungssystem. Erklärungen und empirische Befunde,* 2. Auflage, Wiesbaden: VS Verlag für Sozialwissenschaften

Dietrich, Ingrid & Selke, Sylvia (2007): *Begleiten statt ausgrenzen. Lernbegleitung von russlanddeutschen Spätaussiedler-Jugendlichen an Hauptschulen.* Baltmannsweiler: Schneider Verlag

Eckhardt, Andrea G. (2008): *Sprache als Barriere für den schulischen Erfolg. Potentielle Schwierigkeiten beim Erwerb schulbezogener Sprache für Kinder mit Migrationshintergrund,* Münster : Waxmann

Emmerich, Michaela (1987): *Die soziale Situation ausländischer Kinder in der Bundesrepublik Deutschland.* in Buchkremer, Hansjosef & Emmerich, Michaela (Hrsg.)(1987): *Ausländerkinder. Sonderpädagogische Fragestellungen.* Hamburg: EB-Verlag

Gill, Bernhard (2005): *Schule in der Wissensgesellschaft. Ein soziologisches Studienbuch für Lehrerinnen und Lehrer.* Wiesbaden: Verlag für Sozialwissenschaften

Gomolla, Mechthild & Radtke, Frank-Olaf (2007): *Institutionelle Diskriminierung. Die Herstellung ethnischer Differenz in der Schule,* 2.Auflage, Wiesbaden: VS Verlag für Sozialwissenschaften

Gomolla, Mechthild (2006): *Fördern und Fordern allein genügt nicht. Mechanismen institutioneller Diskriminierung von Migrantenkindern und –jugendlichen im deutschen Schulsystem* in: Auernheimer, Georg (2006): *Schieflagen im Bildungssystem: Die Benachteiligung der Migrantenkinder.* 2. Auflage Wiesbaden: VS Verlag für Sozialwissenschaften, S.87-102

Gudjons, Herbert (1993): *Pädagogisches Grundwissen. Überblick – Kompendium – Studienbuch.* Bad Heilbrunn: Verlag Julius Klinkhardt

Haller, Ingrid (1998): *Kritische Betrachtung der allgemeinen Situation der Migrantenkinder an den Schulen.* in: Kommunale Ausländerinnen- und Ausländervertretung (KAV) der Stadt

Frankfurt am Main (Hrsg.) (1998): *Sonderschulen. Schulen für Migrantenkinder? Hintergründe einer Problematik. Möglichkeiten der Prävention. Dokumentation einer Anhörung am 21.November 1996,* Mönchengladbach: Forum Verlag Godesberg GmbH, S.80-87

Hansen, Georg & Spetsmann-Kunkel, Martin (2008): *Integration und Segregation: Ein Spannungsverhältnis.* Münster: Waxmann

Holzbrecher, Alfred (2004): *Interkulturelle Pädagogik,* Berlin: Cornelson Scriptor

Hormel, Ulrike (2007): *Diskriminierung in der Einwanderungsgesellschaft. Begründungsprobleme pädagogischer Strategien und Konzepte.* Wiesbaden: VS Verlag für Sozialwissenschaften

Hurrelmann, Klaus & Bründel, Heidrun (2003): *Einführung in die Kindheitsforschung.* 2.Auflage, Weinheim: Beltz
Hurrelmann, Klaus (2006): *Einführung in die Sozialisationstheorie.* 9.Auflage, Weinheim: Beltz

Joas, Hans (2007): *Lehrbuch der Soziologie.* 3.Auflage, Frankfurt/Main: Campus-Verlag

Konsortium Bildungsberichterstattung (2006): *Bildung in Deutschland. Ein indikatorengestützter Bericht mit einer Analyse zu Bildung und Migration,* Bielefeld : W. Bertelsmann Verlag GmbH & Co. KG

Kottmann, Brigitte (2006): *Die Überweisung in die Sonderschule. Typische Fälle und Benachteiligungsmuster.* In: Hinz, Renate & Schumacher, Bianca (2006): *Auf den Anfang kommt es an: Kompetenzen entwickeln - Kompetenzen stärken.* Wiesbaden: VS Verl. für Sozialwissenschaften, S.145-152

Langenfeld, Christine (2001): *Integration und kulturelle Identität zugewanderter Minderheiten. Eine Untersuchung am Beispiel des allgemeinbildenden Schulwesens in der Bundesrepublik Deutschland.* Tübingen: Mohr-Siebeck. (Jus publicum, 80)

12

Niekrawitz, Clemens (1991): *Interkulturelle Pädagogik im Überblick. Von der Sonderpädagogik für Ausländer zur interkulturellen Pädagogik für alle ; ideengeschichtliche Entwicklung und aktueller Stand.* 2. Auflage, Frankfurt a.M.: Verl. für Interkulturelle Kommunikation

ohne Autor (2005): *Grundgesetz. Menschenrechtskonvention. Europäischer Gerichtshof. Bundesverfassungsgerichtsgesetz. Parteiengesetz. Untersuchungsausschussgesetz.* 40.Auflage, München: Deutscher Taschenbuchverlag GmbH & Co. KG

PISA-Konsortium (Hrsg.)(2004): *PISA 2003. Der Bildungsstand der Jugendlichen in Deutschland. Ergebnisse des zweiten internationalen Vergleichs.* Münster: Waxmann

Prenzel, Manfred (2007): *PISA 2006. Wichtige Ergebnisse im Überblick.* in: PISA-Konsortium Deutschland (Hrsg.)(2007): *PISA '06. Die Ergebnisse der dritten internationalen Vergleichsstudie.* Münster: Waxman, S.13-30

Radtke, Frank-Olaf (1998): *Interkulturelle Erziehung im Hinblick auf die Sonderschule* in: Kommunale Ausländerinnen- und Ausländervertretung (KAV) der Stadt Frankfurt am Main (Hrsg.) (1998): *Sonderschulen. Schulen für Migrantenkinder? Hintergründe einer Problematik. Möglichkeiten der Prävention. Dokumentation einer Anhörung am 21.November 1996,* Mönchengladbach: Forum Verlag Godesberg GmbH, S.22-34

Sachverständigenrat für Zuwanderung und Integration (2004): *Migration und Integration. Erfahrungen nutzen, Neues wagen (Jahresgutachten 2004),* Berlin 2004

Schröder, Ulrich (2000): *Lernbehindertenpädagogik. Grundlagen und Perspektiven sonderpädagogischer Lernhilfe.* Stuttgart u.a.: W. Kohlhammer GmbH

Seitz, Stefan (2006): *Migrantenkinder und positive Schulleistungen,* Bad Heilbrunn : Verlag Julius Klinkhardt-

Stanat, Petra (2003): *Schulleistungen von Jugendlichen mit Migrationshintergrund. Differenzierung deskriptiver Befunde aus PISA und PISA-E.* in: Baumert, Jürgen & Neubrand,

Michael (2003): *PISA 2000. Ein differenzierter Blick auf die Länder der Bundesrepublik Deutschland*. Opladen: Leske

Statistische Ämter des Bundes und der Länder (2009): *Bevölkerung nach Migrationsstatus regional. Ergebnisse des Mikrozensus 2007*, Wiesbaden : Hessisches Statistisches Landesamt

Stölting, Wilfried (1974): *Zur Zweisprachigkeit ausländischer Kinder. Probleme und Aufgaben.* in: Müller, Hermann & Becker, Ursel (1974): *Ausländerkinder in deutschen Schulen: Ein Handbuch.* Stuttgart: Klett, S.149-164

Treibel, Annette (2006): *Einführung in soziologische Theorien der Gegenwart.* 7.Auflage. Wiesbaden: VS Verlag für Sozialwissenschaften

Walter, Oliver & Taskinen Päivi (2007): *Kompetenzen und bildungsrelevante Einstellungen von Jugendlichen mit Migrationshintergrund in Deutschland. Ein Vergleich mit ausgewählten OECD-Staaten.* in: PISA-Konsortium Deutschland (Hrsg.)(2007): *PISA '06. Die Ergebnisse der dritten internationalen Vergleichsstudie,* Münster: Waxman, S.337-366

Weber, Martina. *"Ali Gymnasium": Soziale Differenzen von SchülerInnen aus der Perspektive von Lehrkräften.* in: Hamburger, Franz et al. (2005): *Migration und Bildung: Über das Verhältnis von Anerkennung und Zumutung in der Einwanderungsgesellschaft,* Wiesbaden: VS Verlag für Sozialwissenschaften, S.69-79

Weiss, Hans Peter (1986): *Interkulturelle Erziehung. Spätaussiedler und Flüchtlinge in der Bundesrepublik Deutschland.* In: Tumat, Alfred J. (1986): *Interkulturelle Erziehung in Praxis und Theorie. Band 3. Migration und Integration. Ein Reader,* Sulzberg/Allgäu: Pädagogischer Verlag Burgbücherei Schneider, S.300-310

Weiss, Karin (2006): *Ausländische Schüler in den neuen Bundesländern. Eine Erfolgsstory.* in: Auernheimer, Georg (2006): *Schieflagen im Bildungssystem: Die Benachteiligung der Migrantenkinder.* 2. Auflage Wiesbaden: VS Verlag für Sozialwissenschaften, S.179-191

Internetquellen:

Demidow, Irene (1999): *Fachlernen in der Zweitsprache Deutsch. Wie zweisprachige Schüler(innen) Physik verstehen.* In: *Zeitschrift für Didaktik der Naturwissenschaften,* 5(2), S. 15-32

Gomolla, Mechthild (ohne Jahr): *Institutionelle Diskriminierung im Bildungs- und Erziehungssystem.* URL: http://egora.uni-muenster.de/ew/personen/medien/gomolla.pdf [Zugriff am 26.01.2010]

Kultusministerkonferenz (1999): *Empfehlungen zum Förderschwerpunkt Lernen,* S.4 URL: http://www.kmk.org/fileadmin/veroeffentlichungen_beschluesse/1999/1999_10_01-FS-Lernen.pdf [Zugriff am 21.01.2010]

Lener, Gabriele (1999): *Schulische Integration und Reproduktion sozialer Ungleichheit.* [URL: http://bidok.uibk.ac.at/library/lener-ungleichheit.html Zugriff am 30.01.2010]

Reißlandt, Carolin (2005): *Migration in Ost- und Westdeutschland 1955 – 2004* URL: http://www.bpb.de/themen/8Q83M7,0,0,Migration_in_Ost_und_Westdeutschland_von_1955 _bis_2004.html, [Zugriff am 08.12.2009]

Statistisches Bundesamt URL: http://www.destatis.de/jetspeed/portal/cms/Sites/destatis/Internet/DE/Presse/pm/zdw/2008/PD 08__042__p002.psml [Zugriff am 02.02.2010]

URL: ftp://ftp.ipn.uni- kiel.de/pub/zfdn/1999/Heft2/S.15-32_Demidow_99_H2.pdf [Zugriff am 6.01.2010]
URL: http://www.gesetze-im-internet.de/rustag/__4.html, [Zugriff am 12.01.2009]

URL: https://www-ec.destatis.de/csp/shop/sfg/bpm.html.cms.cBroker.cls?cmspath=struktur,vollanzeige.csp&ID= 1024589 [Zugriff am 02.02.2010]

URL: http://www.migration-info.de/mub_artikel.php?Id=081002 [Zugriff am 12.01.2010]

Zeitschriften/Zeitungen

Gogolin, Ingrid (2009): *Bildungssprache für alle! Zum Abschluss des Modellprogramms FörMig. Ein Kurzbericht.* in: Pädagogik 2009, Heft 12, S.46-49

Sekundärliteratur

Bourdieu, Pierre (1993): *Die feinen Unterschiede. Kritik der gesellschaftlichen Urteilskraft.* 6.Auflage, Frankfurt am Main: Suhrkamp

Treibel, Annette (2003): *Migration in modernen Gesellschaften. Soziale Folgen von Einwanderung, Gastarbeit, Flucht.* 3.Auflage, Weinheim: Juventa

Angenendt, Steffen (1997): *Migration und Fluch.: Aufgaben und Strategien für Deutschland, Europa und die internationale Gemeinschaft.* Bonn: Bundeszentrale für Politische Bildung. (Schriftenreihe / Bundeszentrale für Politische Bildung, 342)

Gogolin, Ingrid et.al. (Hrsg.)(2005): *Migration und sprachliche Bildung.* in Gogolin, Ingrid & Krüger-Portraz, Marianne (Hrsg.): *Interkulturelle Bildungsforschung. Band 15,* Münster: Waxmann

Brater, Michael et.al. (2009): *Interkulturelle Waldorfschule. Evaluation zur schulischen Integration von Migrantenkindern.* Wiesbaden: Verlag für Sozialwissenschaften

Mehr zu diesem Thema finden Sie in „Bildungsbenachteiligung von Schülern mit Migrationshintergrund" von Peter Dähn, ISBN: 978-3-640-64215-1

http://www.grin.com/de/e-book/152157/

RECLAIMING KINDNESS FOR
THE WORLD OF WORK

THE SOFT STUFF

MATT DEAN

LONDON	NEW YORK	SHANGHAI
MADRID	BARCELONA	BOGOTA
MEXICO CITY	MONTERREY	BUENOS AIRES

DEDICATION

Without Boo, none of this would
have happened. She is everything.

Clem is my dancer, my sense that
we should never accept less.
Herm is my RMs and my Pret,
my sense that we should respect
good things and play straight.
Ned is my sense that we can
all achieve whatever we want,
just by being us (and possibly
playing across the line?)

And Sarah who kept saying
I was her inspiration when it was
the other way round.

CONTENTS

ACKNOWLEDGMENTS   1

INTRODUCTION   3
(The most important moment)

CHAPTER 1.   6
2016, cancer, purpose and love. Trump and *opportunity?*

CHAPTER 2.   24
Climates of fear: a pessimistic view of where we are
right now

REAL-TIME INTERVENTION 1   42
Innocuous white patches, grounding yourself in now

CHAPTER 3.   54
The business case for soft

CHAPTER 4 (PART 1).   74
Unleashing the power of you; individualising and
story telling

REAL-TIME INTERVENTION 2   86
Life is actually about acting opposite to how you feel

CHAPTER 4 (PART 2).   98
Sticking to the diet

CHAPTER 5.   110
You're going to need a tool box. Let's start simple

CHAPTER 6.   122
Making each conversation count

CHAPTER 7.   140
Six more practical tools to help you make this change

CHAPTER 8.   162
Coming to your purpose (aligning it with 'theirs')

REAL-TIME INTERVENTION 3   178
More beardy guru than city boy

CHAPTER 9   188
Integrity is the how; but what actually is it?

REAL TIME INTERVENTION 4   206
I have actually grown a beard

POSTSCRIPT   216
Wrapping it all up in a page (and a half)

ENDNOTES   220

AN INTRODUCTION TO MATT DEAN   224

ACKNOWLEDGMENTS

I want to thank (in order): Helen for asking me where my book was; Michelle for her continual wise counsel and for suggesting I integrate what I was experiencing. Shamik Dhar and his Purple and White Army (who populate the book) including Birdy, Taylor and the Revd Jay McLeod. It would have been nice to mention Al, but I just can't. Jim is P&W and helped a lot with the book. Degs and SMAsher aren't and did too.

Tim, I'm grateful to you for so much. Dame Janet (and John) and everyone, at (or from) S&S, particularly Julian, Anna and Alex all of whom read the proof and cared enough to comment.

byrne·dean and absolutely *everyone* who's been part of what we've done together. I've just written down 50 names and the only ones actually mentioned in the text are VJB, Tim, Kal, Alison and KP. PLMs? As if! Thank you particularly to Victoria, to Janey and to Richard. Without you ... who knows what would have happened. To Uxshely for reading the proof and to Liz, I hope you read this and know.

To Kathryn for being you, Jessie whose clarity was inspirational at an important moment book-wise, to Sharon,

Carolanne, Sarah J, Michelle M, Elaine, Ian and Angus. Also to Nick (who never got paid – just like the rest of you!).

Then (cancer-wise) there is the incomparable Kate who came into work on the Saturday I saw the place and the day after too when it got a bit serious, and Cyrus who's presided over the easy bit! Also to absolutely everyone involved in my care in Brighton and at the Marsden in Sutton and Chelsea. I can't single out individuals but Matthew who ran the now demolished cancer unit at the Royal (where I learned more than anywhere else in the world) – you literally define inspiration. All of you probably understand your purpose?

Also to all of my clients and to everyone who's been in every group, session or audience I've done since I started this gig in 1999. I have absolutely loved it.

Finally to Maddie and to everyone at LID.

INTRODUCTION
(THE MOST IMPORTANT MOMENT)

Early in the morning of Saturday, 22 August 2009 I saw the place in the world where all good comes from. Nearly four months into agressive treatment for head and neck cancer, I was alone in a bed at the Royal Marsden Hospital, Sutton.

I was immuno-suppressed (with no resistance whatsoever to infection) and weakened by chemo and radiotherapies. My blood pressure had collapsed and I was running a temperature of 40-something. I'd been enjoying a crazy light show of dancing neon shapes on the back of my eyelids; probably the drugs.

I learned later that my wife was preparing herself mentally to give our boys bad news. I was, characteristically, in denial. I just wanted someone to turn on the bloody air-con!

Suddenly I felt a faint breath of air on my skin and was deeply grateful. My mind flitted to the prisoners of war in Second World War jungle camps we've seen in films.

Then, the place was suddenly there: clear, golden and bright. It was in the corner of the room but, strangely, a long way away. I knew immediately that it was the place where all good came from and that I could go there. I also knew that getting there would be an effort. I surveyed the place from my bed. I don't remember making a conscious choice, I just left it there.

Before now I have told very few people about my experience that morning. But while writing the final chapters of this book, I realised that properly understanding that moment and that place could be the stone on which I build the whole edifice.

The first time I told someone else about the place was, perhaps, a year after I'd seen it. Whether it was because the person I told was religious or because, by then I'd come to accept I'd been close to death that day, I confused myself into thinking that I had seen something like heaven.

Now, years later, I've come to see the heaven thing as a distraction. The place had nothing to do with death. It's what I first understood it to be: it's where good comes from. The more I've learned about the extraordinary subconscious power of the brain, the more I've come to see the place as a creation of my limbic brain. The place exists inside me.

What's really exciting is that I'm a normal person and if this place is inside me, it's inside you too. It's inside everyone. It's inside the people I struggle to reach out to. Am I just lucky that my first cancer showed it to me?

Perhaps I'm doubly lucky that some of the things I write about in this book: my second cancer; my related mental health problems; and, indeed, sticking with writing this book have helped me to understand more about the long, hard slog we all need to undertake if we're going to make good use of this place that's inside us.

From a place of clarity, and having written the book, I now see what it's about and who it's for. Fundamentally it's for anyone who has thought (perhaps during the sort of sessions I've run in the last decade and a half) *I really want to change what I do* and who hasn't been able to. If you can find your place, your humanity, you can use it as your spark. There are tools and ideas to help you.

Also, because we live in an increasingly fractured world, it's a book for anyone who's alarmed by society's polarisation and wants to do something positive; who doesn't want to wake up in a few years and feel like you've been sleepwalking through seriously changing times. It focuses on what you can do in your own life and particularly in your own workplace. How do we find the humanity and kindness within ourselves to create something more productive and less polarised? How do we change our behaviour to allow that?

You might already be a leader, you might want to become one. I've got a view, by the way, that we are all leaders. You might just be someone who feels helpless watching increasing fractures and polarisation in society and wonders what you can do.

It's a book about doing something to challenge what's become normal for you and changing the workplace you inhabit.

The ideas were formed before *#MeToo*, but they're ideas whose time has come.

CHAPTER 1.

2016, CANCER, PURPOSE AND LOVE. TRUMP AND *OPPORTUNITY*?

I started writing this book at the beginning of 2017. I set out writing about how normal people, you and I, can react to our rapidly polarising times. How we can feel we're doing something useful and positive about the obvious, gaping divides in our society. I think and write about workplaces and leadership. My main focus was always likely to be *what can you do differently **at work** to help heal society's divide?*

It's taken longer to finish than I wanted, for reasons we'll go into. In that time, Brexit and Trump became more normal, *#MeToo* happened, and the divisions in society and the need for each one of us to reach across the divides became even clearer. Because the big thing that my 2009 cancer had taught me was that **love is all that matters**, I set out wanting to explore how we can use love to bring about a transformation at work and in society.

As I grappled with the book, I also struggled to cope with what was happening in my own life. It dawned on me just how difficult it is to bring about even small changes in ourselves and how we behave. So I decided to bring what I was experiencing in real time into the book. These became the Real Time Interventions (there are four). It's what I was experiencing as I wrote. By being honest and realistic and telling my stories, I hoped to provide insight and perhaps to enable you to bring about the small changes in your life on which any transformation in society can be built.

My starting point for the book was that if populism prevails, our political leaders' role is largely to peddle only the most popular ideas, not to provide moral leadership. In that world it will be for others to set the standards on things like humanity, respect, and ethics. The sad truth is that in recent years workplace leaders have hardly excelled in areas like ethics. So, that means there's a real opportunity for others: maybe for you to stand up and be counted; to display and champion the humanity, respect, and ethics that democracy can't guarantee once populism takes hold, lies abound and social media promotes bullying boorishness.

The most exciting part of this is – and this feels like I'm borrowing from populism itself – that every one of us has the power to be a leader and the power to influence others.

We just tend not to.

I wrote the preceding three paragraphs in early 2017, before *#MeToo* showed how people had a voice, and demonstrated the real power that individuals could have in bringing about social change. Without in any way belittling people's efforts in providing their *#MeToo* disclosures, I have a sense that taking to social media was possibly the easy bit. It remains to be seen whether the individuals who did that can follow through and deliver lasting change.

Social media certainly appears to offer normal people an opportunity to shape the world. However, there's a reason why, in his farewell speech as President,[1] Barack Obama said:

If you're tired of arguing with strangers on the Internet, try to talk with one in real life.

Obama's big fear was that each one of us would continue to think that we're making a difference when we shout into the chamber of social media. In fact all that we may be doing is what my Dad annoyingly used to call *the other thing*. Here, that would mean that by shouting into the chamber we're actually keeping our heads down and disengaging from the political process.

Earlier in that final speech Obama had said:

For too many of us it's become safer to retreat into our own bubbles, whether in our neighbourhoods

*or college campuses or places of worship or
social media feeds, surrounded by people who
look like us and share the same political outlook.*

It's important to me that Obama didn't list workplaces as bubbles. Once upon a time, churches, trade unions, and political parties may have been the obvious channels through which people could bring about change. Today, a reducing few of us engage with the world in those ways. We spend most of our time at work.

Most of us work with people who don't share our every outlook. Work is one of the few places where we can engage with others who hail from outside our bubble. Again, we just tend not to hear or to listen to them.

As I've tried to put into words why we tend not to take a lead, not to influence others or even just listen to them, I keep coming back to the same thing: normality and the **power of normal**. We do what we're used to doing, and we see things in a way that suits us. When I use the word sleepwalking, this is what I mean.

In the wake of populism's rise, I have been pointed in the direction of the work of Hannah Arendt, the German-born, Jewish political theorist. She wrote about the banality of evil (how the unthinkable became normalised) and about how the rise of Nazism in Germany was enabled by the people who did *not* support the Nazis – but neither did they oppose them. In her powerful phrase, those people became internal exiles. Their exile involved tending their allotments and looking after their families.

I'm sure all of us have absolutely felt the temptation to do that, to pull up the drawbridge and focus on our own personal surroundings. My simplest message is this: we can't become internal exiles. Whichever side of the divide we're on, we can engage. Where better to start than at work?

MY DAY JOB

I know workplaces and particularly workplace problems. I've been looking at problems that develop there since 1989. Since 1998 I've talked to thousands of people in their own workplaces in 28 different countries. I've basically told them, *you can improve the bit you influence.* My big idea is creating kinder, fairer, more productive workplaces by focusing on what's often called the soft stuff; the people stuff, how individuals at work *feel* and what motivates them.

It has always struck me how happy many leaders seem to feel, admitting in front of their peers: *I'm just not very good at the soft stuff.* They would never say the same about financial stuff or the client stuff. But apparently, it's fine to be clueless about dealing with people. I see the people stuff as the hard stuff. Hard in the sense of difficult. I get it wrong constantly. Also, hard in the way it directly drives the bottom line numbers. We'll look more closely at that connection in Chapter 3.

While talking to those thousands of people around the world, I've developed many straightforward ideas about leading people and driving positive change. A lot of those ideas have found their way into this book. An increasing interest of mine is in people who have been labelled as bullies; I'm often told that my one-to-one conversations with them have quite an impact.

With a self-confessed workplace harasser and bully[2] taking up residence in the White House, and with the Harvey Weinstein allegations developing while I've been writing this book, the focus of my work has possibly taken on a new significance. In that context, I should possibly add a few words about the people I've met who've been labelled as bullies. After listening to them for a couple of hours, the vast majority of them don't come across as evil. They appear to have no malevolent intent.

I've come to see almost all of the people I meet as **accidental bullies**, people who didn't set out to cause the problem(s) that now surround(s) them. Their main failing is simple: they've never focused on the impact they have on others. Their normal is to prioritise their needs and to focus on delivery targets. In pursuit of those targets they adopt behavioural styles they've probably seen modelled by others. This adoption of behavioural styles, of course, takes on a new dimension when the Western world is being led by a proud, self-proclaimed pussy-grabber.

Listening to the tapes by the way, it doesn't sound like Trump's transgressions could be categorised as accidental. And Weinstein? I haven't looked in detail at the allegations made against him, but it certainly looks like he knowingly abused his power – and that the people around him facilitated that (which we'll return to).

THE CANCER THING (AND LOVE)

In 2009 I was diagnosed with head and neck cancer. If you're someone who's had a difficult and a negative experience with cancer, can I please appeal to you now. In 2009 I set out on a personal quest to be a positive cancer role model, to show everyone I came into contact with that cancer need not be negative. This book is written from that perspective, and if you don't want to give that a go I respect that, and I suggest that you abandon this book now.

I've mentioned that the brutal treatment (aggressive chemo and radiotherapies) apparently nearly killed me and that one lasting impact of my diagnosis was positive and simple: I found out that love is the only thing that truly matters in the world.

How did the realisation happen? One beautiful summer evening in late June 2009 I was in bed at home recovering from five days' aggressive chemotherapy. The windows were open, the sun was shining, and I wanted to get up and go across the road to the park. I could hear people enjoying themselves, I thought there might be two games being played in the sun. I wanted to watch.

Over the course of an hour or so, I realised I simply couldn't get up. I had no energy or strength. This was a new experience. I've always done pretty much what I wanted to do. However, on that evening I had the calming sense that it didn't matter. That sense developed because my friend Jay was helping me to join the dots. We were exchanging emails and getting quite deep. He told me the words Christians use on Ash Wednesday: *you are dust and to dust you return.*

I've heard many people say how a potentially terminal illness often helps you see things differently, with more clarity. That evening, by focusing on Jay's simple words, I realised I was OK with missing out on much more than what was going on over the road. I became surprisingly relaxed about possibly missing out on the rest of my life.

The sense of equanimity and calm centred on a feeling of abundance within me. I saw my privileged position, how much I'd had to enjoy in my life to date. What calmed me above all though was not so much my privilege in terms of being a middle class, Oxford educated, white bloke; that's just who I am. It was my privilege in terms of the love I'd been lucky enough to give and to receive through my life.

I suddenly understood that it was love and love alone that would live on (in the minds of others) when I returned to dust. By extension, love was actually the only thing that really mattered. It felt very simple. It *is* very simple.

My experience suggests full recovery from life-threatening illness requires you to face down your own mortality with equanimity: calm and composure. Seeing both my privilege and all the love allowed me to do that. I'd gained new wisdom, everything surely now would be different.

It wasn't enough! It's never enough just to see your privilege, you've got to do something with the knowledge. In 2010, I got back to running my business (too quickly). I did my work and contributed to providing for my family. I made the occasional speech about work-life balance and came out as a workaholic. People said nice things, but I did nothing in my working life about the importance of love. I changed very little.

Writing this book, the biggest questions I've asked myself are principally about how individuals (you and I) can motivate ourselves to bring about change. How we can hold ourselves accountable (to ourselves and to what's important to us). The idea that keeps arising in my narrative is that life doesn't make it easy for us to change anything. Normal becomes a strong power of inertia. If we're going to stop daily, repetitive challenges coalescing into the stuff we always do, then we need to do something out of the ordinary.

In 2010, I had a very powerful motivation and a strong sense that something must change. Then life got in the way and my normal took over. My cancer experiences in 2009 weren't enough to create the lasting change that I hope writing this book can finally represent.

PURPOSE AND ME; A VERY LONG COURTSHIP
Things I wish I'd known far earlier in my life:

that when it comes to fulfilment,
purpose is basically everything.

That simple phrase took me over an hour to craft, and the process felt important! It was the word fulfilment that proved so elusive. What's the simplest way to measure how you're doing in life? I think I chose fulfilment because it's so simple; you know when you're fulfilled. Having chosen it, I could immediately feel how having a clear sense of purpose would have allowed me to be more fulfilled in life. I would have been able to tell myself *this is what I'm measuring myself against*. Without this measure, I've experienced a regular, gnawing sense that I wasn't doing enough good.

I'm a 54-year-old bloke living with cancer. It may be a bloke thing, but writing the first chapters of this book, constructing my narrative, I've found myself focusing (involuntarily) on the question of my achievements. It's unsettled me. If I'm honest, it's unsettled me for years. Because I've never allowed myself to focus on the achievements that really matter. It's never been my personal achievements, my marriage, my relationships with my boys, how I've handled my cancers.

Always, the (unsettling) focus falls on my career achievements and choices. What's this about? I've really struggled to understand this question while writing the book. Because I can see how important the question is and that I need to answer it. I'm also very conscious that nearly a decade ago I was handed the answer. My second cogent thought on being first diagnosed with cancer was absolutely about this. I sat there in the room with someone I'd just met, staring at the label on his tie (Harrods) which was turned towards me.

What I saw with absolute clarity was that I'd spent most of the last twenty years worrying about and being exercised by stuff that really didn't matter. As I recovered, I may have told myself that love was all that mattered. But no-one told the little people in my brain. My normal involved patterns of negative thinking about what I'd achieved (given where I started). My normal was just too powerful, it continued.

Fulfilment is clearly a better measure than achievement. It's certainly far simpler; you know when you feel fulfilled, and good comes from that feeling. If I'm honest, I haven't felt properly fulfilled throughout large tracts of my adult life. My unease has been created by a negative internal narrative centred on, you've guessed it, career achievement.

One clear way of dampening down the negative chatter may be to have a clear purpose and to believe that that really is what it's about. Strangely I think I knew about the importance of purpose in my early or mid-20s. I just didn't pause for thought or stop for long enough to put my purpose into words. Or perhaps I wasn't brave enough to do what something deep inside was telling me to do?

I've now simplified what I think about purpose. There are two elements: (i) our individual purpose and (ii) congruence. Our individual purpose is what Nietzsche called our *why to live*:

He who has a why to live can bear almost any how.

Simon Sinek (with 39 million views[3] of his TED Talk *Always start with Why*) has popularised this simply as *our why*. He may have focused primarily on how firms like Apple should market themselves, but it works just as well for us as individuals.

The idea that on a given day you'll have a bolt from the blue that imbues your life with purpose and value is frankly ridiculous. But I absolutely see the power of purpose and the clarity it can bring. Without purpose, you're at risk of sleepwalking. Possibly very happily, possibly not. If you work at it, if you can distil your purpose down into a simple idea and if you keep that idea at the front of your mind, you'll be able to concentrate your energy, a bit like a magnifying glass concentrates light rays.

The second bit is straightforward: once you're clear about *your why*, you need to make sure you're in a congruent setting, working in a firm or organisation whose purpose is congruent to yours. I develop these ideas further in Chapter 8. The basic point is simple:

> *unless you're clear about your individual*
> *purpose and in a setting that enables that*
> *purpose, nothing will ever feel quite right.*

I was a bright kid. I went through grammar school a year ahead and I graduated from Oxford with a good degree. I started work as a Graduate Trainee (Marketing) on the Unilever Companies Management Development Scheme in September 1986. I lasted just over two years.

I'd done a law degree. In 1988 I decided to return to the law. I'd been quite good at it. The fact that I'd burned all of my notes the day after I finished college (because I'd hated the subject and wanted done with it) was what we might now term an inconvenient truth.

I reasoned that a job in the law would be more task-based and would suit my skill set far better than one in marketing or advertising. I also saw being in the law as a job with built-in meaning. Surely, ensuring that people act in accordance with society's rules would always trump pack design for meaning. The naivety of youth.

So, 18 months later I found myself with a City law firm. I know that probably means something to you that it didn't to me at the time. I hadn't stopped to ask myself what the firm stood for.

I became an employment lawyer; discrimination and harassment were the only things on offer that ever interested me. I acted for employers rather than employees. It never felt right. I assuaged my guilt by volunteering to work at a law centre in the evenings and weekends. I applied unsuccessfully to many firms doing employee work. Not many of my letters were answered. In the one interview I remember, the interviewer kept returning to the fact I wouldn't like the drop in salary that a move to his firm represented.

I did well, I was seen as a rising star at my firm and, through longevity and commitment, ended up as Chair at the law centre. But, as soon as talk turned to partnership at the firm, I ran away. Very ineffectively; I joined a similar firm doing exactly the same work. I justified the move to myself, and anyone else who asked, as offering broader legal experience.

As a 54 year old I think the real reason I left the first firm is clear: congruence. I didn't feel at home with what I did every day or with the setting of a City partnership. Talk of me becoming a partner made my unease with the first firm impossible to ignore. The purpose of both firms, if I even thought about it, was to make money for their partners. It may appear strange that I chose to join another, similar firm. I hadn't worked out that their purpose was the issue. At least moving put off being asked to become a partner.

Through the late 1990s, with my second City law firm, I experienced a literally continuous internal dialogue about not belonging and not wanting to be part of what was happening around me. The dialogue started when I woke up, it came with me on the train to work, it was in my mind during conversations with colleagues. That doesn't help you become more effective or welcomed by your colleagues.

By now, of course, I had family responsibilities. My unhappiness at work became part of my normal, just something I lived with.

After a few years, thanks to an inspired piece of inclusive leadership,[4] I took the opportunity to do (non-legal) work that I genuinely loved; talking to people about the working environment they were creating. Things got better. Things really improved though when I left the law firm and we started our own firm.

The very first thing I did, having decided to create a firm, was to write out its values and #1 was *making a difference*. No-one told me to, nor did I read anywhere that the firm had to have values. I just knew that it did. I think I was becoming a bit clearer too about my own why. Although, if I'm honest, I didn't do any work on it. It seemed enough that the firm had a purpose that I shared (as co-founder).

Looking at things very simplistically, until my first cancer intervened we had a great time. It was hard work, but hard work is fine, particularly when you are an (as yet undiagnosed) workaholic. With hindsight, even in this new setting, had I clarified my individual purpose and worked harder to ensure that the firm was genuinely values based, I think things could have been even better. It would have been easy, of course, to align the firm's and my own purposes (because in theory at least I controlled one and as co-owner, I could influence the other).

THE SUMMER OF 2016

On many levels, the summer of 2016 was when everything changed. It all happened very quickly. I was diagnosed with a second cancer. Weeks later I had a ten-hour operation to remove the diseased part of my tongue and replace it with a flap taken from my wrist. A couple of days before the operation the British people voted narrowly in favour of leaving the European Union.

I wrote at the time (and still genuinely believe) that, given a choice, I would have chosen cancer and a vote to remain in the EU over no cancer and a vote to leave. Of course, we don't get those sort of choices; I got what I saw as the lose-lose option – a second cancer and a leave vote!

As I recovered from the (successful) operation, the media reported an upsurge in bullying across UK society; abhorrent racist and homophobic attacks apparently unleashed by what some called our *Independence Day*. It became apparent just how divided our society was; just how much people like me (surrounded in our bubbles by other people like us) hadn't been listening.

I struggled for a narrative that made sense to me. I needed one because it felt like I'd finally smelt the coffee: if I failed to seize this second chance to do something genuinely worthwhile, I'd be a flawed human being and would die unfulfilled! I visited a broiling August New York to talk to young bankers about ethics (using my new tongue). The place felt somehow already changed. Maybe it was the change in me, the new tongue, and a reduced confidence?

As autumn 2016 unfolded, people like me watched in horror as an unabashed bully, someone who would apparently do away with the sort of workplace protections we regard as our birthright, and who used language that would be unacceptable in the meeting rooms we've inhabited these last 30 years, was given *the* pre-eminent position of power.

I was already in a vulnerable emotional state following my surgery, experiencing extreme mood swings. Like many others I went into some sort of mourning, possibly into internal exile, afraid to read the news. The question I didn't want to know the answer to was: *what happens when a bully gets the pre-eminent position of power?*

When I work with people labelled as bullies, there has always been, at the very least, an understanding that their employer is against bullying. A position reinforced by policies and statements from the CEO and others. We'll delve further into whether this is just a fiction in Chapter 2.

At the end of November 2016, I attended a book launch with many of the UK's top diversity and inclusion professionals. Good, well-meaning people who stand for and create change in their organisations. I was surprised by how normal everyone and everything seemed. The first question to the panel was about Trump. The answers conveyed a real sense of not knowing the impact he would have, but one answer suggested that his election represented an opportunity to us as an industry.

Over the next few days I reflected on what opportunity I could see (if any). Those reflections triggered this book. I hadn't previously seen the places in which we work as agencies of social change or the people who work there as potential protectors of all we hold dear. But then I hadn't heard elected leaders bragging about fondling women, shouting about building a wall and banning Muslims from entering their country. I hadn't previously felt that my government couldn't be relied upon to underpin the protections I treasure.

How should we properly respond to what was happening? I came up with an answer: **each one of us must champion the humanity, the respect, and the ethics that society can't promise us if populism takes hold.**

That could transform our workplaces and society too.

LOVE IS?

*Love is the only force capable of transforming
an enemy into a friend.*

Martin Luther King Jr

Please *really* think about Dr King's words. As opposed to doing what I often do when I'm reading, I just note that there's a quote there!

My central premise from 2009 is that love is the only thing that matters. I've always been wary about using the word love in workplaces. I've heard it used embarrassingly more than once by leaders in an attempt to inspire others. Humanity, empathy, and respect are all good workplace proxies for love. Used wisely, they're also virtues that have real impact in workplaces.

In showing another person love, what you actually show them is humanity, respect, and empathy.[5] That's how you treat the people you love. You might, in fact, view love simply as a motivation, a vehicle for displaying humanity, respect, and empathy to another person. You could have either fallen in love with that person (i.e. chosen to love them) or they may have been given to you, for example as part of your family. What I'm keen to explore is what happens when we choose to display those virtues to other people at work and elsewhere?

Days after Trump's election I met someone who's had a profound effect on me, who brought humanity to life for me. Jo Berry's Dad was killed by the IRA in the Brighton bomb attack in 1984. Jo decided that to make an enemy of his killer would diminish her own humanity. She focused first on her humanity (what I'll define as the quality of being humane, kind, and benevolent), and then she went to look for the humanity of the man who had taken her father's life.

She went to meet him and describes very powerfully how, at their first meeting, she overcame him.

She talks about how he came into the room righteously. This man who took bullying to a new level, who killed people for disagreeing with his beliefs. Jo described how her listening and her empathy literally disarmed this man, how, in time, he apologised for what he had done and how, gradually, they became friends. Jo's message was simple: we should reach out to the person we find hardest to listen to; we should use empathy as a tool for conflict resolution.

I immediately thought about the impact that this sort of empathy could have on the workplace discord that I work with on a daily basis. And more broadly, of course, how it could be used to heal the divides that are opening in society.

We have powerful tools at our disposal.

CHAPTER 2.

CLIMATES OF FEAR: A PESSIMISTIC VIEW OF WHERE WE ARE RIGHT NOW

In the process of writing this book the Weinstein allegations, #MeToo, and #TimesUp all occurred. As someone who's spent two decades focused on creating workplaces where people feel comfortable speaking up, I don't want to get too excited. My sense and my hope is that we're entering a new world. One where people are more willing to speak up and observers are more willing to be supportive and to listen to both sides. The following chapter was written pre-#MeToo. Where I think my words require post-#MeToo comment, these have been italicised.

Many of the large corporates where I work have expended real effort in recent years focusing on the soft stuff. In its current iteration, this is normally a focus on changing the wider culture of the firm. Expensively assembled cultural messages are displayed throughout offices. They implore the reader to act with integrity, passion, or absolute client focus. We'll look later at how I think many firms have failed to cascade these messages. Their intent, however, is clear.

Before this focus on general culture, the previous decade or so saw a focus on diversity and inclusion (D&I). I was there in the early days (at least in the UK) of the push for D&I. With a post-2017 analysis in mind, it's interesting to analyse how the D&I thing arose. Remember, I worked as a corporate employment lawyer, primarily focused on discrimination.

I'm probably bound to say this, but to me it seems pretty incontrovertible that most firms' initial commitment to D&I was risk based. Equal Opportunities and Harassment (or Dignity at Work) policies started to appear because firms were being sued for discrimination. Just look at how we drafted those policies. Many have been changed since, but the legislative (anti-discrimination) language is still plainly there.

The idea of a business case for D&I, that more inclusive firms and those with diverse leadership outperform their competitors, arrived much later. In the early days, the move towards D&I felt defensive and, as a result (probably), many leaders struggled to embrace it. Leaders were sent on mandatory courses. Running those courses often felt like missionary work.

We were working with people who had an established way of doing things and that way worked. Why should they change? There were some converts, but there were many sceptics. There was overt resistance. I'll never forget a senior leader in one firm declaring in one session in 2004:

Look, I've come and I'll stay all morning because I've got to. But you're not getting me to f***ing take part too. I went out drinking last night specially and I feel like sh*t.

I'm interested to know what happened to people like him. Not all of them have disappeared and, since Trump's election, we hear more from them in our discussions. They talk about political correctness, they question whether the old ways aren't in fact the best, they point out that the leader of the free world doesn't appear to be on-message.

A recent[6] high-profile example of this sort of questioning was James Damore's memo circulated at Google, suggesting that women may be biologically less suited to the developer's role. Google's response to Damore's memo was to fire him for advancing harmful gender stereotypes – this gave the issue greater prominence and stoked international debate on the subject.

Diversity and inclusion have certainly become increasingly mainstream in large corporates over the last decade and a half. I've spent a large part of my career talking to senior people in those settings about these ideas. Latterly, I've come to question how deeply those individuals hold those ideas and, by implication, how deeply their organisations hold them. I have started to wonder if commitment to D&I is just something that important people say.

EXPLORING THE SCHISM IN TODAY'S CORPORATES

There's a plurality of views on the soft stuff. It's starkly demonstrated when I sit down one-to-one with someone (normally a senior person) who has transgressed the firm's people policies. You could call many of these people bullies. I seldom, if ever, use the word; such is the intense (negative) emotional reaction it generates. For now, let's call them transgressors. It's certainly how they see themselves.

The transgressors are an interesting group. Before meeting me, any transgressor is likely to have been through the stress of an investigation, perhaps also a disciplinary hearing. They will have come to the unpleasant realisation that their transgression could have ruined their career; that they might lose their livelihood. Of course, if I'm working with them, they're staying in the organisation (for now). Firms don't often pay me to try and reform people they sack.

However, at the very least, a transgressor who works with me will have realised that their transgression may have been career limiting. Having come to this realisation, most transgressors I meet appear somewhat chastened, but they typically display emotions of regret and annoyance rather than contrition. They know they've transgressed the rules, but normally there is neither sincere remorse, nor an immediate desire to change.

There are probably complex reasons behind this. Fundamentally though, I've come to think that they don't believe they've broken their organisation's real, unwritten rules. The unwritten code. I think some of them sit down with me knowing they've got to say the soft stuff is important

– that's the deal. But what they're really thinking is that they're doing the right thing – making their targets.

As I read this with a post-#MeToo lens, I wonder whether this is the part that will change. My early experience is that, perhaps, it has. Maybe people are just waiting for things to settle down again post-#MeToo. Thinking that things will soon revert to being as they were.

All transgressors spend the first part of any discussion with me doing the same thing: justifying their behaviour from their own perspective and explaining things in a way that suits them. Almost all of them focus on one thing. Some start even before we've sat down, before I've set out the context for the session:

> Matt, I know why I'm here but you've got to understand just how badly [the person] was performing.

Performance is where they go first because it's *the* thing, it's the main item in the unwritten code. The early part of a discussion with a transgressor follows a common pattern. They are basically saying:

> Look I understand that I may have been a bit harsh on them, that they may have had something to complain about. I accept that, **but** you've got to understand that this is a high-performing culture; we're all under real pressure to perform.

The transgressors I meet often come from, what has been disparagingly called in D&I circles, the permafrost layer (of middle management). Of itself, the phrase is instructive and I think it shows at the very least a failure properly to understand the positions occupied by these so-called permafrost middle managers.

The name arose because the people responsible for prioritising the soft stuff genuinely believed that, however hard they tried to bring about change, whatever they did, they simply couldn't influence the behaviour of people in this layer. The reality as I see it is rather simpler: this layer is focused on one thing – delivery.

I love the idiom, *they can't see the wood for the trees*. It could either mean that they can't see the larger entity, the collection of trees that make up *the wood*, or it could mean that they can't see the wood, the thing that each individual tree consists of.

The simple truth is that transgressors, together with many of their middle manager colleagues, can only see trees – for which, read targets/objectives/numbers. They struggle to see the big picture (the collection of trees that is the wood), nor can they see the thing that the trees are made of, the thing that's responsible for delivering the targets/objectives/numbers (the wood) which is how their people are feeling.

A CLIMATE OF FEAR

I'm normally hugely impressed by the most senior leaders I meet. That's unsurprising really. You don't get to that sort of position if you can't impress external stakeholders like me. Many of them convince me that they genuinely understand what we are calling the soft stuff. The real question, though, isn't whether they can persuade a willing acolyte in 30 minutes that they understand the importance of focusing on people. What matters is how they actually behave day-to-day.

Some years ago, I worked with a charismatic CEO who I shall call Graham (it's not his real name, because he doesn't come out of this story that well). Graham convinced me at our first meeting that he understood the importance of inclusion. He told me a childhood story of his own exclusion and explained how he used that understanding to guide him in his interactions with people.

As I dug deeper and spoke to Graham's reports, a different picture emerged. Some of his direct reports talked about Graham in a manner that was uncannily similar to the way he'd described himself. They were the ones who had adopted Graham's own narrative. Others talked about Graham as someone who genuinely *saw himself* as an inclusive leader, but who had become too involved in managing the detail, and who ran a firm that was relentlessly focused on numbers.

One of Graham's direct reports told me that if you're phoned for an update on your numbers numerous times in the final week of the month, it doesn't really matter what fine words anyone uses – everyone knows that it's the numbers that matter. These phone calls made the unwritten code explicit, whatever the policies and the glossy statements said, whatever Graham said when he was interviewed.

More recently I've worked with a Divisional CEO over a longer period. I'll call them Sam. I'm clear that Sam genuinely believes in the importance of focusing on people rather than numbers, indeed that became Sam's mantra. We failed to deliver on that mantra though. Sam summarised the idea of schism really well for me in a discussion we had with Sam's direct reports.

Sam expressed the view that the firm could say what it liked about valuing people, but they would never be able to take the people in the firm with them as long as the firm treated people badly when they left. Sam ran a large chunk of a bank. When workforce reductions occur in places like this, the culture is very simple: people leave there and then; they carry away boxes of possessions. We've all seen the footage.

The point Sam was making was that, for so long as people knew that was how they would be treated if the numbers didn't add up, there was little point in trying to build an inclusive, diverse, or people-focused culture.

Because, when push comes to shove,
they know it'll be a black bin bag.

A phrase often used by people in both Graham's and Sam's organisations was that there was a climate of fear:

I see fear everywhere. It comes, I think, from us
being a very performance driven organisation.
People are afraid of losing their bonuses.
They are trying to avoid punishment.

My sense is that this quote could have come from any number of firms or organisations. It doesn't seem to matter whether I'm working in the private or the public sector - even in large charities – although, of course, people there tend not to talk about bonuses. Nor does it seem to matter whether the leader perceives her/himself to be inclusive.

Larry Hirst is a former Chairman of IBM Europe and a very compelling speaker. He spoke at the book launch I mentioned in the previous chapter. He talked about (bravely) addressing a culture of bullying in the corporate setting of IBM and about making a speech in front of his new boss and hundreds of managers at a big corporate get-together.

At the get-together, Larry read out figures for harassment and bullying complaints over the previous year. He then committed to the crowd, which probably contained dozens of alleged transgressors, that he personally was going to make sure that each complaint was properly resolved; that he was going after the bullies. That sort of leadership and the detailed follow up that someone like Larry would have delivered is, of course, what's needed if culture change is going to happen.

I mention Larry mainly because it was from him that I learned some really insightful language. He correctly identified that there is diversity in all organisations. This becomes almost a self-evident truth once you accept that everyone is an individual and unique. Larry accepts that there is even some diversity at the top of many organisations. However, notwithstanding that apparent diversity, Larry's view is that most Western corporates have, for decades, been run from the alpha end of the various spectra.

Larry is saying that only a certain type of person can make the grade, that a dominance of alphas means a tendency to prize certain traits and behaviours – things like effective problem solving and a focus on results. I'm instantly reminded of a series of quotes about a third CEO. Two of this CEO's direct reports said something very similar about him: they explained that the CEO absolutely loved diversity and being surrounded by people of various colours and ethnicities, people from different countries etc. But the direct reports said that it only worked if those diverse people were people like the CEO, people who prized delivery above all else.

In conversation, this CEO said that they prized other things; that they liked supportive leaders who sought and who listened to different perspectives. But I came to understand that that was just something they said in conversation with people like me.

I think that, intellectually, many people share that CEO's position (and sometimes I fear that I may well be one of them). We understand that supportive leaders, people who listen and who seek different perspectives, *should* be more successful. However, we don't measure our people on how supportive they are, or on the number of different perspectives they seek. We measure them on their results.

LEADERSHIP FROM THE ALPHA END

What does being at the alpha end of the various spectra look like? It's about being confident and competitive, having presence and seeking dominance. It's about focusing primarily on results; not being distracted from your objectives and not being afraid to upset people if that's what's required to get the job done. Someone at the alpha end will be strongly task-oriented rather than relationship-oriented.

Female leaders can be alpha just as much as male leaders; gay leaders just as much as their straight colleagues; introverts just as much as extraverts. I could go on. Larry Hirst illustrated the point with a fascinating story about how, working in the new South Africa – the Rainbow Nation of the 90s – he came to see it as a state being run by a set of alpha men and women *of colour*, as opposed to the group of white, alpha males they had replaced.

I mentioned task or relationship orientation. It's a fascinating dimension and the central element of a cultural awareness tool I often use. An interesting question to ask someone is:

If you're meeting someone for the first time and you're going to work closely on a big project, how much time will you set aside in that first meeting to the soft stuff?

If you're genuinely task-focused, a normal answer might be:

Thirty seconds, tops.

A different answer, from a genuinely relationship-oriented person might be:

Well you wouldn't normally talk about the project until the second or third meeting.

I'm not saying that one answer is right and the other wrong, I'm just outlining what being at the alpha end of various spectra looks like.

Cross-cultural research shows that people from places like the US, the UK, and Germany – who, coincidentally, have held the reins of power for the recent period of corporate history – are likely to be far more task-oriented. A number of Asian, African, and South American cultural norms are more relationship-oriented.

For the purposes of this book, what interests me is the question of whether you can change your position on this spectrum; whether we are looking at alpha *behaviour*, or innate alpha personality, or personality traits. My premise is that everybody I work with understands that a person can perform at a higher level for someone who treats them with humanity and respect. However, alpha behaviours become ingrained or normalised.

Currently, there seems to be little appetite for change amongst the people in firms who could make a difference. Because the prevailing performance culture in those firms makes it very difficult to prioritise how people feel. *Again, I ask, is #MeToo going to change this. Possibly.*

It's really up to you.

THIS ISN'T JUST ABOUT HOW PEOPLE IN FIRMS TREAT EACH OTHER

The alpha thing, the competitive wanting to dominate, translates into how firms behave towards their customers and other stakeholders. So many scandals vie for the title of biggest ethical car crash: the Volkswagen emissions scandal of 2015–2016; Enron's collapse in 2001; Bernie Madoff's elaborate Ponzi scheme in 2008; and, as I've written this book, the alleged harvesting of data by Cambridge Analytica.

Just taking one of these examples: programming cars to emit up to 40 times the amount of harmful emissions in real world driving when compared to laboratory test results. How did this happen exactly? There is clearly something seriously wrong with a culture that allowed it to happen. But, perhaps, the example feels a little removed. Decisions about that level of programming will surely be limited to a relatively small group of people (who I visualise wearing white coats).

So, what about the frankly amazing scale of events reported from Wells Fargo, one of the world's largest banks by capitalisation. Wells Fargo was fined $185m in September 2016. The scale of that wrongdoing needs to be considered. Apparently 5,300 employees were sacked after it was found that some 2.1 million[7] accounts had been opened in the preceding years without the customers' knowledge or permission. Customers who, as a result, often ended up paying unnecessary fines and interest (it's reported commonly running to more than $1,000 per customer).

In order to open these accounts, bank workers created phoney email addresses and PIN numbers. The motivation was simple: the accounts enabled workers to satisfy sales goals and earn financial rewards under an incentive programme (that has now been abandoned). One quote from an employee included in the attendant press coverage captures exactly what was going on:

They warned us against this type of behaviour.
But the reality was people had to meet their
sales goals.

To be clear, these people were not the extravagantly paid, master of the universe types from an investment bank. They were people making a living as financial advisers. It's easy to categorise their wrongdoing simply as personal greed. But they were working in an atmosphere of fear: they felt they had to meet their sales targets. To them, meeting those targets justified opening new accounts and applying for new lines of credit on behalf of unknowing customers; real people who would obviously and inevitably lose their own money as a result.

I assume that most Wells Fargo financial advisers wouldn't have felt justified simply taking money from the accounts of their clients. But how different was that to what they were doing? This was not an isolated incident. Similar things happen in modern corporates often enough so as to be unremarkable. Who's responsible?

US Senator Elizabeth Warren, interrogating the CEO and Chairman of Wells Fargo, John Stumpf, is available on YouTube and makes compelling viewing. Warren places the blame squarely on the senior leaders for creating a culture of fear. In my mind it starts with them and extends down the chain, to everyone in the organisation. We're all leaders.

I often work with banks and talk about ethics. I'm introduced by Board Members, CEOs, and Heads of Compliance. I hear these very senior (usually) men who run global banks talk about the importance of ethics and accountability. They use the right words, in the right order.

But as I have sat in the audience with thousands of young bankers, it somehow hasn't felt to me that those words had real impact.

Anyone who has done presentation skills training knows about Albert Mehrabian's work from the 1970s; the idea that only 7% of a message's meaning comes from the words used. No-one I've ever talked to believes the number, but it's incontrovertible that body language and tone are critical too. As is the context in which the words are being said.

To me, this sort of ethical message feels similar to D&I and other cultural messages. They have become part of received corporate speak, they are just things senior people say. I recently spoke to a group of emerging leaders in Singapore about owning a message. The group identified their own leaders as being very weak; they saw that the main reason behind this was the adoption of bland words that meant little; they called this corporate speak. We persisted and identified a complete failure of those leaders to individualise the message, to make it theirs.

It feels to me that ethical and cultural messages don't make it into the unwritten code; in part because leaders deliver unconvincing messages and their followers don't see the ideas being lived and breathed. If we're talking about banking, where ethics are central and where I've spent a lot of time, the message I want young bankers to hear could sound something like this:

*I'm very senior and I've got here because I've been lucky and because I have always acted ethically. For a banker, **ethics is everything**. Without them, you are nothing. Asking people to invest in a bank without ethics is like asking them to give their money to a stranger.*

If you're ever in any way unsure about how to behave, don't do it! Or, before you do, please come and talk to me – I'll make time for you because this is the most important thing we do.

I then want that leader to tell a compelling personal story that demonstrates their point. We'll come back to the importance of storytelling.

Then comes the really difficult bit: any senior leader who has given that message always needs to act as if it's something that they actually believe in, they need to act with integrity (which we'll also come back to). They need to both be seen to act ethically and to talk about the importance of acting ethically. Finally they need to make themselves approachable on the subject.

I can just about imagine some of the people I work with giving that type of message about ethics. I struggle to imagine many of them giving this type of compelling message about initiatives to increase the number of senior female leaders or to improve social equality. I've started not to believe that many leaders genuinely think that, unless their diversity and inclusion initiatives are successful, the firms that they lead will be lesser; that they will struggle to compete.

Maybe this is why we are having so much difficulty in increasing the number of women and people of colour in boardrooms or removing social inequality in firms. Maybe saying that this sort of initiative is important is just something that people in positions of power do. Maybe they're not things that those people genuinely believe in or see as critical.

"WHY HAVE WE GOT A WOMEN'S NETWORK ANYWAY?"

Perhaps it runs deeper than a lack of belief in these ideas? Are there less palatable reasons for D&I's failure of traction? People like me (well-meaning adherents pushing the soft stuff) don't like to talk about this sort of thing, but I've always been genuinely shocked by the rancour that many people at the alpha end of the spectrum (and here I would include both men and women) display when they talk about women's networks.

Over the last decade, almost all of the firms that I've worked with have established a variety of resource groups or networks representing various populations within their workplace. I always assumed that the resentment towards these groups would wane, but apparently it hasn't. I regularly get asked whether I can imagine the outcry if a firm set up a men's network and didn't invite women. I always ask whoever has raised the question whether they think the firm actually needs a men's network and then I exhort them to start one.

It's becoming increasingly obvious to me that the people at the alpha end of various spectra currently in positions of power (most of whom are men), aren't going to give up their privileged positions without a fight. A story I recently heard from a colleague suggests that the alphas will be supported in their fight. The colleague is Head of D&I for EMEA in a major corporate, and was at a social event with, amongst others, a woman she had known for many years and had always perceived as sensible.

The woman had worked in the corporate world before having children. My colleague was amazed when, after a few drinks, the woman started to berate her and the D&I profession for ensuring that the woman's son would be unable to land a good job. He would soon be leaving a good university with a good degree, but she knew that the good jobs would be earmarked for women or people of colour. I've assumed that the mother (and the son) were white.

The more I think about this story, the more I see that it's a microcosm of what's happening in geo-politics. The mother is fearful and protective of her family's position. She has heard something that could be categorised as fake news; namely that it will soon become impossible for able white male graduates to gain the best jobs. Just as I'm interested to see what percentage of terrorist deaths are caused by Islamic extremists travelling from foreign countries, I would be interested to find out how many well-qualified men will lose their jobs or not be given opportunities in the coming years.

I quoted Barack Obama's final speech in Chapter 1. His comments are very relevant here also:

Increasingly we become so secure in our own bubbles that we accept only information, whether true or not, that fits our own opinions.

It's undeniable that there is a significant group in society and, by implication, in the workplace, who believe that the identity of white men is under challenge. I would argue that it's their hegemony that's under challenge. The fake news position is that any hegemony white men may have enjoyed disappeared long ago and that the group itself is now under fire from politically correct forces hell-bent on shackling business.

Michael Kimmel's book *Angry White Men*, was inspired, according to his *TED talk*,[8] by his appearance on a TV show called *A black woman stole my job*. In his remarks on the show he focused on the word *my*. What made that job the preserve of white men? Surely everyone's entitled to work? Addressing that sense of entitlement is important.

A big part of this, Kimmel explains, is to recognise the privileges that we have. He jokes that men in Europe and the US are the beneficiaries of the single most effective affirmative action program in the history of the world. That program is – the history of the world! We'll return to notions of privilege in Chapter 7. This chapter set out to be a pessimistic view of where we are right now, rather than the detail of what needs to happen. One thing's clear to me though: we need to engage white men in the discussion about D&I, now!

REAL-TIME
INTERVENTION 1

INNOCUOUS
WHITE PATCHES,
GROUNDING
YOURSELF IN NOW

I'd written the first two chapters of the book. Obviously, they didn't look anything like they do now; I'm an inveterate tinkerer. But they were written. I'd told Helen, the woman who prompted me finally to write this book, that I'd let her see them when I got back from my work trip.

I was in a hotel room in Singapore. It was Monday morning. Looking in the mirror, I noticed two white patches on my tongue. My phone's camera roll is peppered with tongue selfies. The patches bore a resemblance to the patch that became my tumour in 2016.

I didn't panic. I'd had a few similar things before 2016, one of which was biopsied. They weren't anything to worry about. But last year I hadn't worried either. And a month or so after finding something that looked like this, that thing had grown into an angry looking, unpleasant sore eating away at the side of my tongue. I felt unsettled, like something unpleasant was hanging around me.

It was fine, probably because I was busy and busyness fills the mind. I ran my sessions and put the patches out of my mind. When I arrived in Mumbai on the Tuesday night, I was unnecessarily hard on the hotel receptionist. How could they call themselves an airport hotel and not have free transfers to the airport? If you're that receptionist and you're reading this (which is highly unlikely), I'm sorry. I don't think I'd been 100% successful in putting the patches out of my mind!

I got home at the end of the week. Wherever the patches had been in my mind, once I was home, possibly unconsciously, a desire to share my burden took over. My wife reacted; I reacted to her reaction; we fed off each other. We sent photos to my consultant. He said that the white patches would probably resolve themselves before our planned consultation in a couple of weeks. That had no impact whatsoever.

I spent the next couple of weeks in a state I'd describe as emotional dislocation. It was hard to concentrate on anything.

Without the full schedule of a busy trip to distract me, a pall of negativity hung over everything I did. My negativity centred on the need to provide for my family, and on the impact further absence and tongue impairment would have on our business. The negativity spiralled easily. I grew increasingly tired.

I remember thinking that I might be running down the street to meet trouble. I tried to maintain perspective, but spent a long time pondering what sort of surgery may be required and how debilitating it would be. I sent my consultant more photos and told him the questions we needed answered. He did his best to manage our (over) reaction by email. There wasn't much he could do; he couldn't say there was nothing to worry about until he'd seen me. Anyway, even if he had said that, I wouldn't have believed him!

When we saw him, I knew almost as soon as he looked in my mouth that there wasn't a problem. He gave an expert, technical explanation about recurrence; proximity of the patches to the previous tumour; and the passage of time. But doctor-patient cancer conversations are just like any other human interaction, and you know when someone is unconcerned. If you have faith in that person, that's all you need.

I felt an immediate and massive rush of relief. Biopsy results confirmed no problem a week later, but I knew then. The following day I was absolutely wiped out, I think fatigued by the emotional swell.

A couple of weeks later, having reflected on the experience, I felt embarrassed. The whole episode was so completely unnecesary. More importantly, I hadn't adopted my mantra, my simple rule for dealing with my cancer. Right from the start, that has been ***deal only with what's in front of you now***.

It's easier said than done, but it's the only way I've been able to deal with my cancer. The more I reflect on my mantra, the more I see that it doesn't just apply to cancer-related uncertainty. In any potentially stressful or difficult situation, breathe deeply and think *what do I actually know?* Then deal with that and nothing else.

This incident was so manageable. What did I actually know? I knew that there were a couple of inoffensive looking white patches on my tongue. I knew that my specialist was saying they would probably resolve themselves in a couple of weeks (consultant speak for *nothing to see here*). That was it. Had my mind cast neither forward (to more disfiguring surgery) nor backward (to what happened last year), there would have been no problem.

I hadn't adopted the mantra because in life it's much easier not to stop and think, not to take control of a situation, not to be mindful. It's much easier, so much more normal, to get carried away in the moment, to allow automatic negative thinking to play out. In the work I do, working with employment problems, I see people doing it every day in their workplaces.

I've resolved to develop my equanimity and think it's probably something that many of us could usefully focus on; showing greater calmness in possibly difficult situations. Going forward with my tongue, if I don't develop more equanimity, I'm probably going to spend months, possibly years, in a state of emotional dislocation swathed in a pall of negativity.

It's all about countering our minds' natural inclination to cast both back and forward. Casting back allows the mind to imbue what's happening with greater meaning, using your previous experiences. However, that experience could have no relevance whatsoever. Casting forward, at least for me, is typically in negative spirals. My patches story shows that both can be harmful. So, don't do either!

As I reflected on those weeks following the white patches, on the need for greater equanimity, more focus on what's actually happening now, and more control of the mind's castings, the simple words formed: **be grounded in now**.

People with a diagnosis like cancer often talk and write about the sudden clarity with which they see the world. I certainly bored people on that score! About seeing the beauty in everyday things, in the sky, the breeze, the frost, roadside flowers, or the water droplets on grass. That's certainly part of being grounded in now: noticing what's happening around you, experiencing and enjoying it. There's more to it though: more about controlling your mind.

In the weeks following the white patches, many people said to me that worrying is surely only human nature. I don't view that phrase benevolently; human nature is just the bundle of cognitive biases we've collected and the social norms we've chosen to adhere to during our lives.

You can rise above human nature if you choose to do so.

Somewhat embarrassingly when I discovered the patches I was in Singapore working with groups on how to handle uncertainty and change. The main idea we came up with was, probably, that handling uncertainty is about *taking control*: something I completely failed to do.

Something else compounded my embarrassment: a couple of months before this I'd been taught exactly how to resolve the conflict I was experiencing with a potential recurrence of my cancer. Under the expert tutelage of Jo Berry (who I mentioned in Chapter 1), I'd learned how to avoid exactly the sort of problem I've just written about. Immediately after working with Jo, I'd talked and written about how the exercise we'd done together was a breakthrough moment. I knew then that if I did what I needed to, I wouldn't have to struggle with uncertainty over things like the patches.

Why then did Jo's lesson not come back to me until after the whole thing was over. Because I wasn't holding what Jo had taught me in the front of my mind. I hadn't done what I needed to do to embed the learning. I admonished myself for being basically too lazy to put the learning into practice. I can see why some people say I'm too hard on myself; lazy is a harsh word.

In fact, my failure to embed the learning probably just comes back again to the stifling power of *normal*. We act how we've learned to act; unless we breathe and take control, unless we can overcome the unconscious mind's desire to cast backwards and forwards.

What Jo taught me was a really effective and personal dispute resolution strategy. I make no apologies for going through the exercise in detail here, because it's both so simple and so effective. People who read early drafts of this book split between those who really loved reading about the exercise and those who were turned off by it. If you choose to skip to the beginning of Chapter 3 your enjoyment or understanding of the rest of the book will be unaffected.

Jo normally works with disputes within families, at work or between groups in society. I chose to use the technique to look at the dispute within myself. Of course, as I've proved, the technique can only show you *how* to resolve conflict. It's up to you whether you choose to invest the time and effort necessary to do that. You may choose, as I did, to react in a normal manner when a conflict first arises and allow it to play out normally.

My experience of Jo's exercise was as follows. We all worked with a partner – my partner was a total stranger called Emma. Jo told us to take a handful of beads, baubles, and trinkets from a box she carries with her. Some of you are probably already thinking this sounds a little New Age.

Bear with me, physically mapping out the conflict with these trinkets made it far easier to analyse.

Jo told us to think about an ongoing dispute that we were involved in. As I've said, I chose the ongoing dispute I have with the idea of my cancer's recurrence. Emma chose a dispute with someone she worked with. I sensed that Emma felt her choice was prosaic or workaday in comparison to mine. That was simply overcome by compassion; by me showing kindness to Emma, reassuring her that if it was causing her stress it was something we should discuss.

Jo gave each one of us a few minutes in turn, in which one of us talked, uninterrupted, about our dispute. As we were doing that, we also mapped it out using our trinkets, explaining to our partner what each item represented. Our partner's role was just to listen, empathetically. The partner was allowed to ask questions, but only to help our understanding. Their main job was to *really* listen.

Talking to a complete stranger, who is being 100% supportive and listening intently, is a very strange and hugely invigorating experience. It certainly affects the energy with which you approach the telling. When I was playing the listening role, about a minute into her explanation Emma suddenly said, *this is confidential isn't it.* She'd realised quite how much she was divulging to a complete stranger!

There was also a real novelty to representing a dispute visually. I experienced an unusual clarity of thought during the exercise. After five minutes, the photo over the page is what I'd set out on the chair between Emma and me. The large shiny bauble in the middle is me. The pretty button touching it is my cancer, or at least the threat of its recurrence. I carried that button in my pocket for some weeks afterwards. The orange lamp (as far as I remember) was a warning light related to recurrence. The buttons and the shell to the left are other people, onlookers.

I talked for those few minutes about my inner most thoughts. I created the picture. Emma paid attention to what I was saying; her empathy and understanding were palpable.

I then listened with (I hope) empathy and interest as Emma told her story. The experience was powerful for both of us. At the end of the session we discussed how bizarre it was that we had made such an immediate and deep connection.

What Jo did next was, for me at least, totally unexpected. She just said:

OK, you've got two minutes to solve your own puzzle, to reposition your baubles. Your partner's role again is to just listen to you.

I went first and I saw almost immediately what needed to happen. The rearranged picture looked like this. You possibly can't see, but the shell and the button representing my cancer are now balanced (a bit precariously) on top of the bauble representing me. Actually, the cancer button sat in the shell opening really well – that's why I chose the shell for the role. The onlookers have become supporters and are below me. I think that the lamp now represents the direction of travel.

The agglomeration of the shell, the cancer button, and the bauble that's me need some explanation. [That, by the way, is not a sentence I would ever have predicted writing!]

The shell has now become my emotional self. It's clearly part of me and so it sits on top of the silver bauble that represents me. The cancer button sits on top of the shell because in the resolved state my emotional self has welcomed, it has made peace if you like, with the idea of recurrence. At the time of explaining this to Emma I knew exactly what that would involve.

I should explain that, for as long as I remember, I have been prone to low-level anxiety and poor sleep. Since my initial cancer treatments those anxieties have increased and I have tried (with help) to develop strategies for coping with them. One technique I learned in 2015 was focusing, welcoming anxiety rather than pushing it away and over-coming it. To push the anxiety and sense of panic away was my instinctive response (and probably the response every-one else has).

I have learned that if, somewhat counter-intuitively, I welcome the strange fluttering sensation that appears in the darkest reaches of my stomach, good things can follow. A couple of times I've had some limited success with the process. I have visualised the fluttering anxiety as a timid animal that needs to be enticed out into the open. I've come to learn that it's there for a reason, it's got something to say.

In the two minutes I spent rearranging the baubles and explaining how to resolve the problem, I realised that I needed to do something like that with the threat of my cancer recurring. Rather than banishing any thought of it, I needed to welcome it into my emotional self. I have said and written that I have benefitted greatly from the experience of cancer, that it has made me a better person. But that's operating at a rational level, that's weighing things up after the event.

What I saw in a moment of clarity during the exer-cise was that I had never made peace with my cancer, at least not at the emotional level. That, I think, would have involved sitting quietly with my feet flat on the floor, focusing on my breath, and waiting for the idea of my cancer recurring to show up. When (perhaps, *if*) it did appear, I would have had to welcome it, to recognise that it was there for a reason.

Perhaps it would have spoken to me. That's the sort of thing that happens in my mind and possibly in yours – if you create space for it. The fact that I have not yet made that peace means that I will continue to react negatively to patches on my tongue. I need to realign the baubles.

CHAPTER 3.

THE BUSINESS
CASE FOR SOFT

Part of my role over the last decade or so has been to keep on top of the growing body of research supporting the view that focusing on how your people feel is good for the bottom line. This chapter isn't in any way exhaustive. It's some of the stuff that's convinced me, which I use to convince others.

A good place to start is with Gallup Inc. Their **State of the Global Workplace** series, based on data collected globally with clients using their Q-12 engagement survey, is compelling. In 2008, they published a very simple piece of research.[9] I have shown the resulting diagram to many business leaders, senior partners, and CEOs. They all react in the same way.

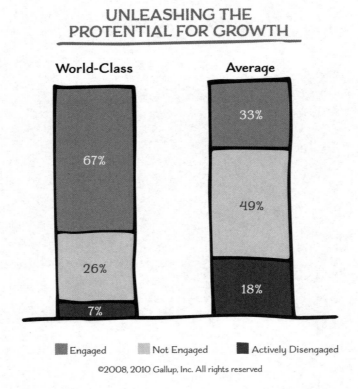

UNLEASHING THE PROTENTIAL FOR GROWTH

World-Class	Average
67%	33%
26%	49%
7%	18%

Engaged   Not Engaged   Actively Disengaged

The diagram shows that those clients whom Gallup rated as genuinely world-class in terms of their objectively rated overall performance had a workforce with approximately two-thirds (67%) of workers engaged and just over a quarter (26%) not engaged. At this point people generally start asking for definitions; *what do engaged and not engaged mean?* We'll come back to this, but we all know the difference when we see it.

The critical thing the research showed is that an *average* organisation, not one that's performing badly, but one that's doing better than many, has almost half of its workers in the not engaged bucket, and just a third in the engaged bucket. I'm not exaggerating when I say that revealing the right-hand side of the slide often leads to gasps in a room of senior people.

Shortly after this, the person in charge will often say something like *getting two-thirds of our people engaged, surely that's achievable.* It is achievable, but it won't just happen.

To understand how much this research underpins the business case for soft, consider some of the Q12 questions that Gallup asks workers to assess whether they are engaged, not engaged, or actively disengaged:

Q10   – I have a best friend at work.
Q5   – Someone at work seems to care about me as a person.
Q8   – The mission or purpose of my company makes me feel my job's important.
Q4   – In the last seven days I've received recognition or praise for doing good work.

Each worker is categorised depending on their answers to these questions. The questions continue, covering areas such as: whether your development is encouraged and your opinions seem to count; whether someone talks to you about your progress; and whether you've had the opportunity to learn and grow, to do what you do best every day.

At its simplest, according to the research, the more people who answer these questions positively, the more engaged people you have, the more likely it is that you are going be a world-class organisation.

I don't think anyone can prove a direct causal link between happy, engaged people and world-class performance. If you work in a world-class firm, you'll surely be more engaged. Or you could argue that it's the well-run firms, the ones that focus on their people processes, that perform the best. One by-product of that focus on people processes may be greater feelings of engagement.

But there's a common-sense position here: everyone gets that happy people will work harder, that they will have more energy to give and be more committed. Most of the leaders I've worked with have seen this and have resolved to pay more attention to how people feel in their work life.

The same difficulty in proving causality is highlighted in McKinsey's compelling Delivering Through Diversity 2018 report. The extended research conducted globally in 2017 confirms the correlation McKinsey first identified in 2015 between firms with the highest levels of gender and ethnic diversity (particularly at leadership levels) and financial over performance. The more diverse firms are substantially more likely to outperform against the median levels in their sectors. However, no-one can show that the outperformance is actually caused by the diversity. It could be, for example, that high performing firms attract more diverse talent.

The most important recent research in this area has been Google's Project Aristotle. The tech giant invested massively to answer the question: *what makes a team effective at Google?* Detailed data was collected from members of 180 of their teams. Researchers, statisticians, organisational psychologists, sociologists and engineers spent four years working on the question. Charles Duhigg, a Pulitzer Prize-winning journalist and author, wrote extensively about Aristotle for the *New York Times*.[10]

When the Aristotle team started (in 2012), most thinking about team performance focused on the excellent research of figures such as Katherine Phillips, now a Professor at Columbia Business School, into the performance of heterogeneous and homogeneous teams and how diversity (of thought and experience) could add greatly to performance.

The principal finding of the Aristotle researchers (published in 2016) was straightforward: *that what really mattered was less about who was on the team and more about how the team worked together.*[11]

Duhigg explained that the researchers reviewed half a century's academic studies into how teams worked and uncovered much insight into group norms – how groups function when they gather. They searched through their amassed data to identify norms in Google's most successful teams. According to Duhigg it all started to fall into place when the Aristotle team encountered the concept of **psychological safety**. *Of the five key dynamics of effective teams that researchers identified psychological safety was by far the most important.*[12]

In 1999, Amy Edmondson, a professor at Harvard Business School, first referred to **psychological safety** as: *a sense of confidence that the team will not embarrass, reject or punish someone for speaking up* and a climate characterised by *interpersonal trust and mutual respect in which people are comfortable being themselves.*

Duhigg highlighted a fascinating study from a group of psychologists from Carnegie Mellon, M.I.T. and Union College published in the journal Science in 2010.[13] They found that in their tests what distinguished the most effective teams from the dysfunctional was how the members treated each other: that the right norms could raise the collective intelligence. According to the study there were two norms of behaviour that all the good teams generally shared: **conversational turn taking**: *as long as everyone got a chance to talk, the team did well* and **high average social sensitivity**. This sensitivity was measured using a test in which participants are shown people's eyes and asked to describe what the people are thinking or feeling. In simple terms these team members will sense how their colleagues are feeling.[14]

The most effective teams work like this; they display social sensitivity to each other and ensure conversational turn taking. That builds psychological safety. For me, having spent nearly 30 years looking at workplace problems and a decade and a half talking to leaders about inclusion and diversity and working with many dysfunctional teams, this idea of psychological safety, built on those norms makes perfect sense.

In my work before Project Aristotle I talked primarily about whether people in the team felt comfortable in their workplace and able to be themselves. *Comfortable* never quite captured the right mood; comfortable people don't stretch themselves. Psychological safety is different, it describes a base from which people will launch themselves.

Of course, knowing that these simple ideas are critical to team performance is one thing; helping the people at Google, or elsewhere, to create the trust and respect from which that safety grows is a different matter. One story from Project Aristotle's implementation jumps out at me. Duhigg wrote about a senior Googler, Matt Sakaguchi, who was guided by the Aristotle team as he tried to improve his team's performance.

The team had been working together (seemingly quite well) for about ten months and completed one of the

Aristotle surveys to gauge their group norms. Sakaguchi's team scored themselves quite harshly on how well understood the team's role was and whether the team had impact. Bothered by the way that his team had completed this questionnaire, Sakaguchi asked the team to an offsite.

To start things off, everyone at the offsite was asked to share something personal about themselves. Sakaguchi went first and told his team something that no-one on the team apparently had any idea about; that he had Stage 4 cancer.[15] He'd lived with his cancer for a decade or more, but recently it had spread to his liver in what appeared to be a serious development.

In the article, Duhigg recounts how Sakaguchi's admission prompted others to share personal details about their health, or relationship breakups, and how in turn they were able to talk about team stuff that was bothering them, and agree new norms together.

My personal experience absolutely told me that Sakaguchi's sharing would create new norms in the team. The thing I found difficult to understand was that he had not mentioned his cancer to work colleagues for a decade. In 2009, I shared my diagnosis (of my stage 2 cancer) with my team on the morning of the third day. I needed their support, so I needed them to know exactly what I knew. At that point, it was a specialist saying: *it looks like cancer to me.* We didn't go out to our clients with the cancer diagnosis until it had been confirmed, but when it was confirmed we told them too.

I communicated with anyone who was interested (colleagues, clients, everyone in my network) in some detail about the treatments I was facing and how I was feeling. I didn't really differentiate between family and friends and people from the world of work. I have to say that the reaction to my openness is probably best described as an outpouring of positivity. More than one client told me that they loved me.

Many focused on the importance for them (and their organisations) of the work that we had done together.

All of that has had a lasting impact on me. I formed the view then that there is only one you and that you shouldn't try to create work and home personas. You should just be yourself.

On a recent project in an international law firm, working with large groups of people, I asked them to discuss the following question, *what actually happens when you are able to be yourself at work?* There was concern expressed in some of the debates that it might lead to more conflict. However, the general sense was that it wouldn't because, this being work, people would naturally tend to be professional.

Someone tried arguing that genuinely being himself would mean wearing his pyjamas to work. He quite quickly accepted that he wouldn't actually do that. I did, however, make the point that there seemed to be a move in the firm to less formal dress; a senior partner who'd just introduced my session was wearing quite scruffy jeans. Certainly not anything like as formal as I would have expected a partner to wear when I worked in a firm like theirs. Dressing how we want is surely part of being ourselves at work.

The groups generated some really powerful ideas. When you are able to be yourself at work there are fewer distractions; you aren't having to expend effort to be someone you're not. It's also more likely you'll feel that you can trust the environment. You'll be more creative. You'll be *liberated* to perform at your best. That word liberated became very much the central idea of the initiative.

At the beginning of 2015, I was involved in a small discussion group with some serious commentators and big hitters, including a former UK CEO of a corporate leviathan and the incoming Chair of a global bank. About eight of us shared ideas for 20 minutes and I jotted down three quotes which captured much of the discussion for me:

Your life should be about what's important to you.
I always say, get yourself a life and then put work
in there somewhere!
You employ the whole person.

These quotes were from the business leaders themselves, not from any of the lobbyists or commentators who made up the group. I'll leave it to you to work out which was said by the most senior man around the table.[16]

This idea of fitting your work into your life is interesting to anyone who has participated in the work-life balance debate over the last two decades. The word balance has lost much of its resonance. The focus is increasingly on how we work, how effective we are in all we do and how our overall sense of wellbeing will add to that effectiveness.

I think I first heard the idea of *bringing your whole self to work* as part of a Stonewall[17] campaign, highlighting the impact on workplace effectiveness that non-inclusive behaviour may have on members of the LGBT (lesbian, gay, bisexual and trans) community.

In 2002 (probably), I remember being at a fantastic, relaxed social event at a bank I still work closely with. The event was for members of the firm's various employee resource groups to meet socially. I chatted to many people, including Mark who had started the LGBT group. He knew that I regularly spoke to managers at the bank about leading their people. I asked him:

If I say just one thing to leaders about what it's
like to be gay here, or how they should approach
managing someone from the LGBT community,
what would you want me to say?

Mark thought for a while. Then he said: *Please tell them that being gay is not something that I do in my spare time ... it's who I am.* He went on to say how it felt when people said, as they apparently often did (perhaps still do): *I don't care what you do in your spare time.*

Mark's point was that he's always gay, just as I am always a father or in recent years living with cancer. I don't stop doing or being that when I come to work, and I don't think anyone is suggesting that I should. Someone who's told that they can be gay in their spare time is unlikely to feel psychologically safe in their work environment; they may be distracted and have to expend effort pretending to be someone they are not.

ARISTOTLE'S OTHER FINDINGS (AND THEIR OVERLAP WITH DAN PINK)

In addition to psychological safety, Google's careful research into high performing teams published four more differentiators:

dependability: can we count on each other to do high quality work on time?

structure and clarity: are goals, roles, and execution plans clear?

meaning of work: are we working on something that is personally important for each of us?

impact of work: do we fundamentally believe that the work we do matters?

Dependability: I see this very much as a function of the other elements. Psychologically safe team members who see meaning and impact in what they're doing and have structure and clarity to work within the team will normally deliver.

Structure and clarity: I'm going to leave this to others; it's the boring and necessary bit, on which I have little new to add.

Meaning of work: meaning and, to a lesser extent, impact are related to purpose and we will keep returning to this.

Returning to some of the research that's convinced me of the business case for soft, I would add Dan Pink's extremely simple and useful analysis of the research into individual motivation. If you have not seen the RSA's (Royal Society for the Encouragement of Arts, Manufactures and Commerce) ten-minute animation summarising Pink's analysis, I recommend it to you.[18]

In short, Pink has popularised the distinction between extrinsic and intrinsic motivators for work. Extrinsic motivators, like pay or recognition, come from outside. Pink shows that research has consistently demonstrated that, for anything requiring more than basic cognitive function, extrinsic motivation does **not** work as a motivator. Offering a performance bonus does not increase people's motivation. In fact, it may hamper their performance.

Pink identifies three primary intrinsic motivators:

mastery – getting better at what I do;
autonomy – being allowed space to do my thing; and
purpose – being attached to something that's bigger than me.

For the last decade and a half, people in workplaces have talked explicitly about the power of mastery and autonomy. More recently they have started to enunciate the power of purpose.

WHAT I'VE LEARNT ABOUT THE IMPORTANCE OF DEVELOPMENT

When reflecting on their own career, most people don't see something that resembles a measured progression from one point to another. The careers that most people talk about are messier; their levels of engagement, development, progress, and affiliation fluctuate.

I've spent many years getting leaders to focus on and learn from particular moments in their career. Starting with a moment in their working life when they were not developing at all; in fact they may have even been experiencing negative development (going backwards).

I'd encourage you to do this now. Put the book down and focus on a real time in your career; a moment when you were not developing. Think about the characters who were there, the things that you were doing and how you were being treated. Often, people are struck by how easy it is to remember these moments in their careers, or how many of them there are.

In 2006, I worked with a close friend of mine and his senior leadership team. We had a great session and afterwards he provided me with clear feedback:

What really struck me, what I'm taking away is very simple. All of the people in there were very successful, real high fliers. But ... it was the pace with which they were all able to talk about a difficult time in their career. That's the thing that made the difference, isn't it!

I ask participants initially to focus on what actually happened to them; they explore how they were being treated. I've taken a random sample of comments made by participants in a set of sessions in continental Europe in 2015 and set them out below. It's a small sample and nothing like a scientific study, but I've ordered them in terms of how frequently, over the years, I would judge each idea has been referred to.

For example, **lack of challenge** is, without a doubt, number one in terms of the frequency with which it's raised as part of the negative treatment people have suffered. I probably could have filled an entire book with the various notes I've kept, but I doubt that it would have been any more insightful than the list below.

I knew before I chose the sample that the list would be exactly as it is: a simple and quite unremarkable litany of work-a-day experiences. **Boss misconduct** is at number three, but there appears to be just one egregious or Machiavellian example of intentional wrongdoing. This supports my premise that most bullies are accidental; they just haven't focused on the impact of what they do.

The poor treatment experienced by the people I work with normally stems from thoughtlessness, or from leaders falling into patterns of thinking about an individual. A great example of this came recently from a woman who said:

It was like my boss had a 'me-shaped hole';
he needed someone to do exactly what I did.
And strangely, I fitted that role perfectly!

Unremarkable as the list may be, I defy anyone who leads people to read it and not feel uncomfortable about how their people may be feeling. It contains at least one reference to a lack of meaning and purpose (point six).

1. **Lack of challenge**: being taken for granted, doing something absolutely within my comfort zone, facing no challenge. The job becomes routine, the tasks become repetitive. *Been there, done that* or *could do it with my eyes closed.*

2. **Lack of support or relationships with key people**: lack of direction and guidance, lack of presence, lack of personal connection (all pertaining specifically to the boss(es)). *There was no investment in my career progress; No-one took the time with me; I thought she didn't care about me, that it was all about the numbers; He wasn't interested at all in my products; He didn't actually understand or make an effort to understand my role; The manager just didn't have the skills to develop me.*

3. **Boss misconduct**: a wide litany of poor communication and worse, obviously described solely from the perspective of the teller. *He hid things from me; He told me he had no confidence in me; There was no communication and then he was just rude; He falsely evaluated me; He undermined me in front of others; She said 'I told you to do this' when she hadn't; He was questioning my expert knowledge; A mean manager discriminating expressly against my group.*

4. **Micromanagement/controlling**: different people explain micro-management in different ways. *He had an obsession with detail, with formatting; Constantly questioning: where is this, what is that?; We were being controlled; It was very hierarchical – we weren't allowed to speak!*

5. **Lack of clarity**: the person lacking clarity about what they should be focused on. *No clear idea of what was required or what I was supposed to be doing; The goal posts kept moving.*

6. **The role had been overpromised**: the day-to-day reality of the job does not live up to the description sold to them at interview. *I wasn't given the promised access; There just weren't the opportunities I had been promised.*

7. **Not what I wanted**: the person is not engaged on work that they want to do. *They were forcing me to do stuff that wasn't me; I was made to do things I didn't want to do; I didn't buy into the vision.*

8. **Struggling with politics**: office politics are experienced negatively in many settings. *I felt I was being excluded by the new owner; I had to focus on positioning myself every day; Someone else was taking credit for what I was producing.*

9. **Underemployed**: there is actually little worse than the phone not ringing! This can follow unexpected change/ restructure or particular areas or functions may become neglected. *The phone just didn't ring.*

10. **Lack of opportunity for development**: there is little or no opportunity to do things differently. *We always do it this way; You can't do that, this is the cash cow, nothing can put that at risk; I was told to follow orders.*

Having focused on what was happening, it's important to find out how people felt at the moment. I reproduce the list of emotions experienced by people in those same European sessions. It's probably a powerful list; again I've started with the emotions I judge to be the ones that people mention most frequently:

frustrated, bored, angry (angry at my manager), excluded, neglected, ignored, isolated, sad, questioning myself (questioning all the past good things), low self-esteem, lacking confidence, disappointed (disappointed – I wanted to grow), used, looking elsewhere/moving on, demotivated, disengaged, incompetent, a failure, worthless,

unhappy and insecure, irritated, annoyed,
wanting to do better, lost, no purpose, no hope,
no interest, unfulfilled, going through the motions,
disillusioned, dissatisfied, discouraged, fear,
nervous anxiety, not respected, not trusted,
not valued, not appreciated, 'at a roadblock',
misused, abused, **tortured***, shut out, guilty,*
exhausted, very tired, trapped, paranoid,
unrecognised, impatient, 'like an assistant
[not a Head of Group Media Relations]'.

Remember, this is a list of how successful leaders in an organisation have felt at a moment in their career when they were not developing. While I can see its power, I'm unsurprised by the content.

People don't frequently disclose much about their emotions at work, but if I get them to talk about a time in their career (with their current employer or elsewhere), I find that they open up. I remember the person in this sample using the word *torture*. It had a huge impact on the others in the room.

What's critical is that participants recognise that they've been in that place and that they start to relive some of the emotions they felt. With this realisation, and having revisited the emotions and negative thoughts they experienced at the time, can come greater empathy. It's certainly easier for people who've done the exercise to identify with the feelings, thoughts, and, potentially, the attitudes of others who may be currently occupying that place.

With the participants, I build what I call **the employment cycle**.

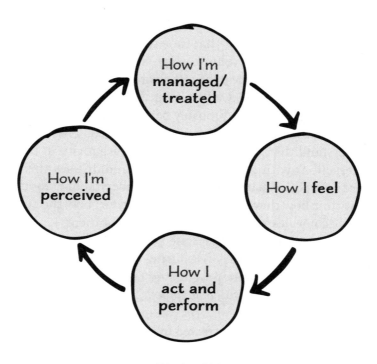

©Matt Dean 2019

How you're treated at work by others is never going to be the only thing that drives how you feel; other factors will influence that and it's the same with each link in the cycle, but participants seldom, if ever, question the validity of the individual connections.

Having talked about treatment and emotions, we move on to discuss how people were performing at that time. Most people want to say that they are, above all, professional and that they would never let their standards slide. However, knowing what they can (and regularly do) achieve or commit, many admit to a five or six out of ten in terms of commitment to their work. Others happily give a two or three (out of ten), sometimes explaining the greater dedication they were giving at that time to other aspects of their lives: family, writing, volunteering – whatever.

Finally, I ask people to be self-aware, to think about how others would have viewed them at that time. Often, they can see that they were probably being perceived as a problem, or as someone to be carefully managed. They might understand that, possibly, they gave off negativity in their interactions with colleagues. They often didn't see this at the time; I think participants may be understanding for the first time how they were viewed at that time; how the cycle had become destructive and debilitating for them.

There's a far shorter exercise you can do to get people to think about how they felt during the moments in their career when they were progressing fastest. They will say: *excited, trusted, energised, bulletproof…* The words fall from their lips.

How were they being treated in that moment? What was happening to them? They give very consistent answers: being given the opportunity to develop something (and themselves); being trusted to deliver; having a supportive boss who would listen and provide whatever support was required.

Participants use the language of Dan Pink, they talk about **mastery** – the opportunity to develop – and **autonomy** – being able to shape how they developed. Sometimes people talk about purpose, meaning, and impact.

You can see (and use) the cycle as a leadership model, something to help you get the best from your people. Or you can use it to help the people analyse themselves and understand the dynamics of the situation they find themselves in.

When we've built the red, destructive cycle in which negative treatment is driving negative feeling and behaviour, I make a point of asking leaders the same question:

*If you see poor performance or negative behaviour,
what's the one thing that this model says you must do?*

I think, logically, it's difficult to answer this question without mentioning the right-hand box; how the person is feeling. I'm struck by how many leaders avoid the feelings box by how they seem uncomfortable just talking about emotions. Is this about not wanting to bring their whole selves to work?

When they answer my question, people talk about breaking the cycle and most focus on the top box: treatment is the thing that they see that they control. They want to change how the person is being treated. It's the same all over the world. My message is simple: to be an effective leader, you need to understand that you have a great deal of impact over how people are feeling and that you need to create relationships with those people in which they feel safe telling you how they feel. You also need to **care about the answer.** You need to recognise the massive importance of feelings in driving behaviour and performance. By the way, no matter where you are in the world the answer to the question, *how's everything going?* seems to be pretty much always the same: *Fine* or *OK.*

You need to ask a better question. You also need not to get stuck on your side of the cycle. Leaders tend to focus solely how the person is performing and their categorisation.

CHAPTER 4
(PART 1).

UNLEASHING THE POWER OF YOU; INDIVIDUALISING AND STORY TELLING

"IF NOT YOU, WHO? IF NOT NOW, WHEN?"

In September 2003, the first piece of paid work I did for our newly formed company was to speak on a residential *managing stress* taster session. The session included some focus on physical fitness, and one of the other facilitators was either Jonny or Greg Searle. I honestly can't remember which one it was (which is dreadful). The Searle brothers won an Olympic gold medal for rowing in Barcelona (1992) with their cox Garry Herbert. They came from behind in the last hundred metres to beat the Italian favourites – literally by inches. There is an iconic picture of Herbert in tears on the podium, dwarfed by the two (far bigger) brothers.

Herbert's job as cox was to steer (down the straight course) and to motivate his colleagues. The point of my story is that I met and spent a Sunday evening and the following day with one of the brothers. I had the perfect opportunity to check with him whether Herbert had actually shouted the words *If not you, who? If not now, when?* to the brothers as they approached the final stages. And if he did say the words, what impact did they have?

I'm interested because in the years since 2003 I've come to see that these words encapsulate so much of the message I've been trying to get over. It's up to the people in a workplace to determine what kind of environment they work in. I want them to see that if they don't do something, nobody else will. If they don't change their workplaces, it won't happen.

The problem though is obvious. In that boat, everyone's minds were very focused. This was the Olympic final. There were two blokes with oars and their job was to propel the boat forwards, very quickly! There was a smaller bloke whose job was to shout at them. As they approached the line, it was now or never, procrastination wasn't an option.

In most of the places I work there is little or no focus on the environment; there are lots of people who could do something if they were motivated and there is absolutely no sense of urgency. I work either with senior people (on their own or in groups) or with whole teams. If I'm working with a whole team they've normally experienced some problems.

The people with authority over the team (or some of it) know that part of their job is to manage or lead. They know that they should be doing *something*. However, as I've said, they will prioritise the rest of their job, the thing that they will refer to as their day job, i.e. delivering on their objectives. Also, they primarily see their management role as the management of individual performance and the setting of objectives. In the language of Project Aristotle, they look first to create structure and clarity.

They tend not to recognise their influence over the mood or dynamic of the team, and the environment people work in. Nor do they recognise just how important the energy that comes from that mood or dynamic is to the overall team performance.

My experience of working with people who have no authority in their teams is that many of them know *what* they could do to help the team function more effectively. They know who they could provide support to, or talk to about their behaviour. They just don't see that as being part of their job; they don't see themselves as being leaders.

So people in workplaces seldom, if ever, see the amount of influence they can and do have over their bit of the organisation, particularly over the dynamic or mood. Nor do they see how critical this can be in driving team performance and effectiveness. The result is that often no-one looks after the team dynamic.

The other thing people miss is that taking the lead can have a really positive impact *on them* personally; it can make them feel more valued and important, and it can create the positive, green, engaged cycles we mentioned in Chapter 3. I think this book is about making sure everyone considers unleashing themselves in their workplace – taking action to improve what's there.

THE LONG, HARD SLOG TOWARDS CHANGE

I described in Chapter 3, how over the last decade and a half I've got thousands of senior people to understand that in one particular moment they were awesome, but in another they were far from that. Also to see how they performed in both moments was all about how they felt – which in turn was affected by how they were being treated.

Having worked on an emotional rather than an intellectual level with those leaders, having got them to think about how they *felt* in those moments, I hope that I've increased their tendency towards empathy. I hope I've made it easier for them to think about and care about how the people around them feel. With the cycle, I've also given them a powerful tool to increase their own effectiveness and the effectiveness of those people around them. What's frustrating is that I don't know what they do when I leave!

The same is true when I work with whole teams. I show teams that each one of them has an important role to play. I provide a framework, a language and some tools they can use. But what will they do next? I can imagine what people do because I know what I've done, even when I've been fired up by a real sense of purpose. I have normally done what I normally do.

As will become clear in the next segment of the book, I've recently been working with a fantastic clinical psychologist called Nick. We only had six sessions together, but his impact was massive. In our final session, he said something very powerful, to which I keep returning:

> *That's why pop psychology books from the 90s*
> *are so rubbish; you can't change your life with*
> *a bit of self-awareness and some goal setting.*
> *Personal growth is a long, hard slog.*

Increasingly, I'm realising that this book is about my own long, hard slog. It could also be about yours (if you want it to be).

As I've written this book and recognised just how difficult it is to bring about change in my own behaviour – when I want to – it's become increasingly obvious to me that it's help with the slog that we need to provide people in organisations. Spending a couple of hours with me might give someone a bit of self-awareness and some goals in Nick's phrase. If you're going to be successful in changing behaviour, there are two elements: getting people to take that critical first step (which I'll call **unleashing**), and sustaining them as they progress; helping them **stick to the diet**. I want to deal with *unleashing* in this part (Part 1) of this chapter, and *sticking to the diet* in Part 2. Before we get there, a few words on social organising because how you might motivate yourself draws on how you could organise others.

MY INTRODUCTION TO SOCIAL ORGANISING

One day in the summer of 2010 a young woman phoned me at work unexpectedly. I took to her immediately. The next day we met and agreed that she would work with us. Because of my legal training, I tend to make notes of every work related conversation. The notes of that first conversation start:

Talking to my Mum.
Want to work for byrne·dean.

That conversation was with Kathryn Perera. In the relatively few years that have passed since, Kathryn has: done some great work for byrne·dean; had two children; been the CEO of Movement for Change (a charity that has helped ordinary people to do extraordinary things across the UK); spent time as a visiting professor at Harvard (where she worked with Marshall Ganz, the guru of social organising); and taken on the role of Head of Transformation at NHS England. We'll return to Kathryn and her achievements (and her Mum) in due course.

Kathryn introduced me to the concept of social organising which has fundamentally changed how I view the idea of cultural change in the workplace. Social or community organising came of age in 2008, when it was fundamentally important in bringing about victory for Barack Obama. It's a powerful force that mobilises people in local communities to organise and hold power to account. It strengthens individual agency (the capacity for all of us to act independently). It's centred on relationships and on developing individual leadership.

Organising is far from a traditional campaign strategy. Organisers – who can come either from the outside or from within a community – act *with* people, not for them. Those people are catalysed or *unleashed* [my word] to bring about change.

Social organising chimed strongly with my view of organisations. It incorporates both my view that we're all leaders and my growing interest in the importance of purpose. I was hooked before I read Marshall Ganz's definition of leadership:

*Accepting responsibility for enabling
others to address their purpose.*

Ganz believes as I do that leaders aren't the people to whom organisations choose to give power and status. They are those of us who choose to influence our peers, to help the people around us to do what's really important to them.

To understand organising properly, it's critical to grasp that our values (which is just another way of saying what's really important to us) are what shape the actions that we take. I see values as being like a software of the mind;[19] they determine how we will act and the things that we will be motivated to change. However, the thing that brings those values to life, what precipitates us to act and to bring about change, is emotion. An emotion is, of course, no more than a chemical message in the body.

Understanding your values and generating an emotional response within yourself will be a critical part of you starting out on the road. To be really effective at getting others to bring about change, we need to generate emotional responses (in ourselves or – when organising – in other people). Relying on this, the theory of social organising proposes that change happens most effectively when human beings **tell stories**. Stories generate emotion in ourselves and others. All of us have a compelling story to tell and one that will move others towards action.

When we tell a story we express our values as lived experience, rather than as a concepts or ideas. Those lived experiences have greater power to move others because they inspire emotional responses. Suddenly I realised that, despite her protestations to the contrary, Kathryn may have started our conversation by talking about her Mum for a reason!

We'll return to the theory of social organising in Chapter 6 when we look in detail at how to make your conversations count. First, let's nail what I'm calling **unleashing**; you taking that all important first step towards bringing about some sort of change.

UNLEASHING – KEEP IT SIMPLE

To unleash the power of you in your workplace, I have three ideas:

1. *Simple, human things matter most – so priortise them.*
    Keep these simple ideas at the forefront of your mind – things like:
    *   *listening to people will make them feel valued;*
    *   *someone's emotional state determines how they behave;*
    *   *the best teams are those in which individuals feel psychologically safe (people are listened to and their colleagues understand how they're feeling).*

    On its own that sort of understanding will have limited value. What matters is whether (and how) you try to put these simple ideas into practice, how you go about creating an environment of conversational turn taking or whatever. Increasingly, I see the main challenge being **to exercise humanity and consideration towards everyone, not just the people with whom you connect most easily.**

2. *Recognise that you have the power to change things.*
    What transforms an emotional spark into a flame that can bring about change is your recognition that you actually do have the power to do something – to change the environment. The emotion may be negative (anger, sorrow or regret) or positive (excitement) but nothing will happen unless you recognise your power.

In my experience that recognition doesn't often just happen; people don't see it for themselves unaided. Normally someone plays the role of catalyst, shows you (or others) that you can be important. Could that be your role: helping others to understand that they can effect change?

3. *Care enough to individualise the simple ideas that matter.* Each person involved in change needs to individualise the ideas involved before anything can happen. In my view, firms consistently fail in change initiatives because they focus insufficiently on how what they call the cascade will work. They carefully choose their values and invest in setting the tone from the top, but they don't invest in effective dissemination, no plans are made for how people will individualise the ideas.

If I want someone to behave in a particular way, let's use the example of acting with integrity, first I need them properly to understand what that will look like. I can only explain what integrity means (and looks like in practice) once I've individualised it as a concept myself and come up with some well-chosen stories to use.

I could have chosen a simpler idea than integrity, for example listening or co-operation. The principle would still apply though: the individuals bringing about change would still need to take time to understand what each of those ideas actually looks like in practice and to think about how they would explain them to others.

Integrity is a good example to use because most firms number it amongst their values and most people think they have it. Yet when asked to explain what it is, few can. I certainly would always have described myself as having integrity, but I struggled to explain it when first asked to do so. These days I often ask people in banking or law to explain what the idea means. They often struggle too.

To individualise an idea, first you need properly to understand it. My test for proper understanding is that you're able effectively to explain the idea to someone else. It's only when you've properly understood an idea that you can share it and have the conversations that genuinely make a difference.

We're all different and we learn in different ways. For me proper understanding involves drawing the idea, normally in pencil. I jot down the component parts and position them together on a page. You probably do it differently.

In connection with integrity, I've done that work now. I broadly know what integrity means to me. My understanding may shift slightly, but I have achieved a proper understanding. I've also done the second part of individualising, which leans heavily on social organising theory. I've selected the stories that I can use to explain what integrity means to me. Interestingly most of them come from my personal not my professional life.

For example, many years ago I got into a bit trouble with my wife because I hadn't shared with her a piece of information (about a mutual friend's marital infidelity). We didn't argue, but when she told me she thought I could have shared the information, I said quite simply: *I couldn't. I'd told her that I wouldn't tell anyone else.*

This (and other) stories really helped me properly to understand my version of integrity. For me, acting with integrity is about me (Matt) **holding myself to a higher standard** than I would expect of others. If I told a friend a particularly salacious piece of information in confidence, I think I'd expect that they might share it with their partner. I don't think I'd condemn them for doing so. If I'm able to keep that information to myself, that satisfies my test of integrity. I will have held myself to that higher standard.

By the way, if you're worrying, there would, of course, be situations in which I could share that sort of information with my wife. I would first want to assess the benefit and damage that would accrue from me doing that. We'll come back to this when we look in more detail at integrity in Chapter 9. I'm just using it here briefly to explain what I mean by individualising.

Perhaps the preceding paragraphs have demonstrated the power of story-telling in culture change. My short story expresses my values (in this case integrity) through lived experience. It's more likely to evoke an emotional reaction simply because it's a story.

Ideas can only cascade or pass through an organisation effectively if everyone individualises them and passes their version of those ideas on to people they influence. If they do that in a manner that generates an emotional reaction in the other person, there's more chance that the next person will change their behaviour. It also helps by the way if the next individual can see both what they have to do and how they will benefit.

At its simplest this is just: understand that you have more impact than you realise, take the time properly to understand a few simple, human ideas and talk to people around you about them (not just the people you connect most easily with).

REAL-TIME
INTERVENTION 2

LIFE IS ACTUALLY ABOUT ACTING OPPOSITE TO HOW YOU FEEL

After the white patches, I accepted that I needed help. I'd been referred to the psychiatric services at the Marsden at the end of 2016 – for what my consultant and I called low mood. I didn't actually seek that help for another six months. I had a good break at Christmas and came back thinking I was doing OK. I probably was doing OK. I was functioning, doing my job, playing a role in my family.

How was I actually? That morning in May 2017 when I went for a psychiatric assessment, I wrote down some simple thoughts about how I was. I also asked my wife to give me a sense of what I was like to live with.

I wrote:
I want to curl up.
I don't feel safe.
My default is to run away – I don't want confrontation.
I haven't achieved.
There's too much to do.
I'm tired.
The business hasn't worked.

She wrote:
Unpredictable mood.
Self-absorbed (it's all about you).
Your reaction to me is all about how you are feeling, not about my need emotionally.
If it's not about you or of direct interest to you, you don't even listen.
Irrational about anything financial.
Sometimes very short tempered.
Can be controlling, then disappointed and annoyed if I (others) don't do what you want or react as you want. Angry if this is pointed out.
Glass always half empty but you're swift to give upbeat

advice to others, as if you know better.

You are chronically sleep deprived.

I read what she sent me on the train as I went up to the Marsden that morning in May. It wasn't easy.

The sleep thing was true. I was waking between three and four in the morning and found it really difficult to get back to sleep. Hours of night-time Sudoko on my iPad seemed like a good way of not letting my mind spiral out of control. On the train, looking out of the window, I thought the rest of it had to be true because it was the impact I was having. I felt sad.

I particularly wanted to see someone at the Marsden who would understand what they refer to as cancer pathways. He asked knowledgeable questions about my drug prescriptions and explained how that could affect mood. He knew about what I was facing, I felt safe in that room.

He opened by telling me that a disproportionately high number of people living with head and neck cancer (compared to other cancers) seek psychiatric support. Probably because head and neck cancers disfigure. I don't think I'm disfigured by the way. I just sound a bit odd and don't have a normal tongue. And your tongue is quite an important, personal part of you.

We talked about current thinking on the impact of trauma; how it seems that people put up with their first trauma and then their second, how they get on with life. The third time though, they may start to think: *is this what my life's all about now?* Even though the white patches weren't actually a trauma, they were! That made sense to him (and to me).

That first conversation had real value for me, a real impact. Importantly I got a diagnosis: he told me I was suffering from anxiety that (he thought) was trauma related.

He confirmed that there was something wrong with me and gave it a name. He also validated that I had been through a great deal. Is it strange that I needed someone to tell me that? I remember particularly liking the fact he used the word reasonable when he talked about how I was reacting to things.

It wasn't actually my first conversation with a Marsden psychiatrist. I admitted this to him. I have a letter following a one-off consultation in 2010. It says that I had returned to work too early and was working too hard. This was in 2010, after my first cancer. We don't learn. Even when the professionals to whom we have gone for guidance and help tell us something. Particularly if it's something about work.

In 2010, soon after my return to work and probably about the same time as that first consultation, I came out publicly as a workaholic. It was part of my manifesto of change; I wanted to do only work that mattered and to spend more time with my family. My desire for change went back to that second cogent thought I had when I first heard that I had cancer: that I'd spent most of the previous 20 years worrying about things that really didn't matter.

I didn't change. Because change is difficult. Particularly for addicts. Bryan Robinson is an academic and prolific author on the subject of workaholism, including *Chained to the desk: a guidebook for workaholics*. His definition of work addiction or workaholism (he says you can choose the term you prefer) makes perfect sense to me:

An obsessive-compulsive disorder that manifests itself through self-imposed demands, an inability to regulate work habits and over indulgence in work to the exclusion of most other life activities.

OCD is a diagnosis and I make no comment on that. However, obsessive is a word I've used in lay terms to describe myself, particularly where work is concerned. Many of my work demands are self-imposed and my attempts to regulate work have always failed. An example: in September 2016, returning to work after my operation, I designated each Monday as a non-working day. That lasted until ... the first Monday (which I worked). For months, each Monday in my Outlook diary proclaimed itself a non-working day. It made no difference to the meetings that were put in – by me or others.

The most obvious example of a self-imposed work demand was my decision to fly to New York to do a talk with 140 people; this was in the seventh week following the operation on my tongue. We talked quite a bit about this decision when I met the psychiatrist. No-one was demanding me to go. In fact, my colleagues and my wife were doing the opposite. But I was insistent. And Cyrus (my surgeon) had said I could go!

For me, the reference to work as an *indulgence* also makes perfect sense. There are other important things I could do, but I work because it's an escape. Robinson explains that work addiction is an escape from unresolved emotional issues. The relief it provides from those issues is what's addictive. Work provides temporary relief and distraction from a deeper condition. If I keep working I can prevent the embers of that condition from developing into a wildfire.

In the weeks following my operation in 2016, allegedly to monitor post-operative (speech) progress, I regularly posted short videos of me talking about my progress (on www.well-disposedcancerist.com). They're an interesting historical watch (at least for me). Others have watched them too. Elaine is a confidante (she's also living with cancer). She noted how much I talked about work in the videos.

I think that she might have expected me to talk about more important stuff? Because I was writing the book I asked Elaine if she could put her reaction into words. She wrote;

When watching Matt grappling with whether
he was taking control of work over the course
of the videos, I wondered if his difficulty reflected
the dual and contradictory roles that work plays
for him: his way of embracing life, but also his
way of escaping it.

Elaine is a pyschotherapist by the way! Over these last few months I've often thought about those dual and contradictory roles. Work is a large part of how I embrace life and it's always been an escape. Before now, though, I had never understood what I was escaping from.

In 2010, when I first considered the issue of workaholism, I wondered what my unresolved emotional issues might be. In 2017 the answer was clear; the psychiatric lead at the Marsden had told me I had anxiety.

However, on hearing that I had trauma related anxiety, my wife's first words were *you've always been like that*. It's true, and I now see that my work addiction has always been a distraction from, my way of living with, my underlying anxiety. By working I kept it at bay.

I've looked again at some of those videos as I started to think about things, like why I went to New York. At the end of week six (after my operation) I said the following:

Hello! End of week six. Time flies by.
I'm back, in the garden ... obviously.
Came back from holiday last night, from Sweden.
Lovely place, lovely holiday.

*Bit daunted, bit scared, because tomorrow,
I'm flying to New York to speak to 140 people
using this voice. Ummm ... It's going to be fine.
No, it is going to be fine!*
I'm feeling good, I'm feeling very good.
I've started physio and this [I point to my neck/
shoulder on right hand side] *has started to feel better.*
There's nothing really troubling me. [I look into the
distance and nod my head] *Yeah ... It's great.*

It's interesting that I chose not to mention a couple of tumultuous rows I had caused on holiday by being what, I can only term (with the benefit of my wife's words), self-obsessed. Instead I chose to tell the world; *I'm feeling good, I'm feeling very good* and *There's nothing really troubling me.*

How ridiculous do those words sound with the benefit of hindsight? Although I think I believed them at the time. Happily, I can report that in the following week I was able to post how well New York had gone. I also assured people:

*I'm not going to rush back into work,
I did that last time.*

You may be thinking that I had just flown to New York for work! I was listening too, at least a little bit. I also said:

Something that Victoria [my wife] *said after
she saw last week's video. She said 'It might
make it sound, to anyone who's looking, that it's
been easy.' But it hasn't been easy at all. I've been
tired, I've been grumpy, I've been all those things.
But I'm really proud, after seven weeks, of where
we've got to.*

Returning to the real-time intervention; about three weeks after that initial consultation, I met with Nick. He's a brilliant clinical psychologist. I've had CBT and counselling before and to good effect. But in 90 minutes with Nick, it felt like I made more progress than I ever had previously. It helped that in the morning, before I met Nick, I had sat down for a couple of hours with Helen.

Helen's a coach. In fact she's written books about coaching. She was helping me with my book and suggested that she might usefully give me a few coaching sessions. So, that day was all about self-improvement. It's the sort of day that can only happen when you admit that you have a problem and need help.

The first goal that Helen and I set that morning was very simple. It was to work less. To have at least two full days each week in which I had nothing at all to do with work. Ideally on those days I would wake up without a plan and choose what I wanted to do. Small steps, but steps that really made a difference to me in the months that followed.

In the afternoon, I met Nick. I immediately loved his self-deprecating, Kiwi style. We connected easily. On the train home, I wrote down what I could already see were my three massive learnings. This in just 90 minutes.

First, I understood why I do the whole controlling thing. Previously I had denied that I even did it. However, in the weeks since my first consultation (and in that room with Nick) I came to see myself as extremely controlling. I seek to assert control over situations and people. Nick made it feel that it was a safe thing for me to embrace. He said it was obvious to him that controlling my environment has brought me a great deal of success. We talked about the trip to New York as being the apogee of my controlling behaviour. I wanted to assert control over my cancer, to demonstrate who was in charge. That's exactly why I went.

Not only did I clearly see that I do it, I got some insight into why I do it. I won't dwell on this here (because I don't think it's that relevant to the narrative), but that understanding has been helpful. We talked about my apparent perfectionism, my wanting things to be right. I imagine I share this with many people. Nick suggested that, as a hangover from my childhood, my limbic system (my emotional brain) is telling me that if the thing I'm doing isn't perfect, something bad will happen.

Remember the emotional (limbic) brain always gets to go first, and is far more powerful than the rational brain. Rationally, I may know (now that I'm in my 50s) that no-one is going to shout at me if people aren't sitting round the table at the exact moment I produce a meal. But my limbic system gets to go first and is telling me: *you know what's going to happen.*

I sat on the train, writing this down, making sense of so much of what I had struggled with for many years. I was working with someone who had simplified things for me.

The second thing Nick taught me that afternoon, and which, for the first time, I genuinely believed, is that we are *always in control of our behaviour.* We can't choose what happens to us, but we can choose how we react to it. We need to treat the limbic system as the toddler that it is.

It seems ridiculous to me that someone who had regularly talked and written about emotional intelligence, about Steve Peters' inner chimp,[20] hadn't yet grasped something so simple. But those words came as a revelation for me. I felt inspired, I actually wanted to control my behaviour.

The third learning followed logically, and was the most powerful. It was that *most of life is actually about acting opposite to how you feel.* Nick drew me a stick person with two paths in front of it. I'm looking at it now (months later). To the right is **how I want to live my life**, to the left is the **fix it/avoid** path.

That second path, the one to the left, travels through quicksand. If you take it, you sink into the quicksand. We all know that when you're in quicksand, you shouldn't struggle, you should do the thing that feels completely wrong: relax and do nothing. It took me a while to understand the name Nick gave this path. I understood immediately why it was the avoid path, the one you took if you wanted to avoid conflict with yourself. What took longer to grasp was that it was also the *quick fix* path too. Which I came to think of as anything other than a proper fix. For me, it became the 'quick fix/avoid' path

I didn't work it all out on the train; that came in the following weeks and months. But that first session was the initial step to seeing that the fix it/avoid path (through the quicksand) is waking early at the weekend and *slipping into the office at six for a couple of hours before everyone else wakes up.* It was actually often before six. I've written elsewhere that I always believed this to be a way of me doing the work I thought I needed to do without impacting on my family.

I'd love to see a video of myself on some of those family Sundays, when I'd done half a day's work before appearing home to cook breakfast. Actually, on reflection, I wouldn't. Those days were, invariably, car crashes. *What do you mean you don't want breakfast? I've cooked it all now!* I just didn't see that they were dreadful, or perhaps I just didn't link their dreadfulness to my workaholic behaviour.

That path also means doing nothing when a colleague says something that makes you uncomfortable; it means getting on a plane to New York when the people closest to you have asked you not to.

On that path, you feel no personal discomfort, because you're doing the thing that feels right, that feels normal. It's the thing your limbic system wants you to do (Nick said always remember that your limbic system is predisposed to avoid *all* discomfort).

Choosing the other path, doing the other thing, the how I want to live my life path, means discomfort. I've been amazed, for example, at just how much discomfort I have felt in taking those two full days off – totally off. It gets a bit easier, but the anxiety in the early days was palpable. The other thing about this path, is that first (as the name suggests) you need to have decided and made explicit exactly how you want to live your life, to have worked out your values, what's truly important to you. Only then can you make informed choices. We'll keep coming back to that!

CHAPTER 4 (PART 2).

STICKING TO
THE DIET

Once you've unleashed yourself, very little, perhaps noth-ing, happens. But, you'll be ready to go. You will have recog-nised that you've got power and that it's the simple things that really matter. You will have invested in individualising some of those simple ideas, making them real for you. But you need to start doing small things differently, probably acting the opposite of how you feel and taking a few steps down the how I want to live path.

You'll also need to keep going along that path, to keep motivating yourself to do things that don't feel normal. If you want to have a real impact I think you're going to need help. I don't think you *need* the professionals that I was lucky enough to have, but without a network it will be very difficult. Are there people who're committed to helping you progress? People who want you to succeed.

This is going to require you to have some explicit con-versations. To start using some of the principles of social organising. The conversations will be specifically aimed at providing you with the support that you need. *This is what I'm thinking about ... Do you think you might be able to help me?* If those are not the sort of conversations you have with friends and colleagues, perhaps now is the time to start.

FIRST, A SIMPLE PLAN?

A simple plan is going to help. In a spirit of individualis-ation, of course, you need to come up with your own plan. I can share mine with you. It developed as I wrote this book. As with most things I create, it has three simple elements:

1. Understand my why (my purpose)
2. Ground myself in now
3. Act always with integrity

Number 1 is how **I want to live my life**; it's a strategic direction that will hopefully prevent me from continually sleepwalking into the quicksand. Number 2 could make progress along the path far easier by reducing unnecessary distractions. Number 3 will guide me whenever I'm faced with a choice in daily life.

In Chapters 8 and 9 we will explore purpose and integrity in greater detail. At this point I want to spend a little time exploring sleepwalking and what (#2) **grounding myself in now** actually means to me (after a few months of trying to practice it) and how I came to use those exact words.

As far as sleepwalking is concerned, it really is this simple: ***unless you know what you're trying to achieve, you can never feel fulfilled.*** Written down, that sounds cheesy and akin to the pop-psychology Nick condemned. The thing is, as someone who honestly thinks that I've slept-walked through much of my life with no clear sense of what's important, I'm starting to understand that a goal could have been transformational. My sleepwalking would be fine if I'd always felt fulfilled, but I haven't.

This feeling crystallized in 2009 when I first heard I had cancer, and more recently during that first psychiatric assessment in 2017 when I was asked:

*If your funeral was going to be in five years,
what would you like people to say about you?*

Of course, he prefaced the question with *purely as a hypothetical exercise.* It just didn't feel like that much of a hypothetical question, sat in a consulting room at the Royal Marsden.

I'd like to think that people at my funeral will talk about stuff that isn't work. But work and what we achieve there is a big part of all of us. We'll return in Chapter 7 to how being yourself at work is a key part of the equation. In Chapter 8, we'll develop this with the idea that we have one life and one purpose. Ideally the purpose that you choose can encapsulate what you do for a living.

I'd just add one more idea about purpose at this stage and it's really simple: *carry it with you, wear it on your sleeve. Share it with others.*

My experience, since I've started to talk about this, has been remarkable. Simon Sinek's, *always start with why* isn't just a way of marketing firms like Apple, it works with people too. Think about what you say and how you appear when people ask you what you do for a living.

Years ago, I was sat next to someone on a long-haul flight. After 12 hours, as we were coming in to land in Singapore, we struck up a conversation (as you do). He was a mining engineer and was being flown out to Australia to solve a problem in a mine where people were trapped or in some kind of imminent danger. I can't remember exactly, but it all sounded very exciting and important.

I knew what was coming next. What would I say I did? When he asked, I came out with *I talk to people about being nice to each other at work.* Without missing a beat, the action man beside me said, *we could do with some of that!*

Reflecting on that story now, I want to know why I didn't make more of it, why I didn't start to see myself as that person, start to feel prouder about what I was doing and creating around me. The answer, I'm sorry to say, is probably about busyness, and about not taking the time to think about what was important. It's about sleepwalking.

WHAT DOES GROUNDING MYSELF IN NOW ACTUALLY INVOLVE?

I was asked recently whether I could relate my thoughts on grounding myself in now more towards the sphere of work. I thought quite hard about this and had a clear realisation; I'm pretty good at grounding myself in now when I'm at work. Probably most of us are.

I'm on the phone to a client, I'm thinking very carefully about what she's saying, I'm listening for clues. It's the same facilitating sessions with leaders or writing a paragraph of a book. I'm focused and in the moment, my mind doesn't wander or let water in.

Workwise, I only struggle to keep that focus when I'm tired (which happens much more often than it used to). The only other time in recent memory I remember struggling to be in the moment was in the weeks after I found the white patches. I described earlier how *a pall of negativity hung over everything I involved myself in.*

Just to illustrate what the pall actually looked like at work, the following is instructive. One day I went to Leeds. I was demonstrating a small part of a session to a couple of people. It was a pitch: the sort of thing I've done dozens of times, unthinkingly and normally successfully. That day I started to stress on the train about not having the right equipment with me. I ran around Leeds trying to buy that equipment (although it transpired I didn't need it). I sat in the reception area and remember inexplicably wanting to cry. I started doing the thing and there was a voice inside my head telling me that I was boring, that I had chosen the wrong part to show them.

We didn't get the job! Because my mind was casting around and letting water in.

I've reflected in Real Time Intervention 1 on how I let those negative spirals happen. In summary, though, this is about the power of the limbic brain to prey on sleepwalkers;

when you choose not to breathe deeply and tell yourself to focus only on the thing in front of you.

In recent years, living in the moment and mindfulness have very much become buzz phrases (at least they have in my bubble). In the aftermath of the patches, I faced up to the task of individualising the idea I'd come up with of grounding myself in now; of properly understanding and then, hopefully, trying to practise my version of it. How do you do that? How do you change a lifetime's behaviour?

My first taste of success with the mantra was during the long months of my cancer treatment in 2009. A period you could classify either as a crisis or exceptional. As soon as the threat passed, I returned to the negative spirals. I can see the irony. As soon as the thing of real concern passed, I started to worry again.

On the day of my first diagnosis, I drove down to see my parents and first my brother. He and I were out walking. I remember he made me laugh by saying: *so you're going to get a payout and lose a shed load of weight, what's not to like?* We also talked about serious stuff. He's an inveterate worrier too, and I was giving him something new to fret about.

I remember saying to him that I knew I would sleep soundly that night for the first time in ages. I knew because there was now only one thing to worry about and it wasn't something that I could control. I did sleep well that night and I woke up feeling as if I was living in a palace rather than the shabby house that needed lots of things doing to it that I'd been living in earlier that week.

The small things could look after themselves. I remember going downstairs and looking at the garden of our palace in the early morning light and thinking that nothing would ever be the same again (in terms of my relationship with that garden!) I then went to find my wife who I found fast asleep on the floor of our little office.

Something I wrote in 2009, two and a half weeks after diagnosis is worth revisiting. *I've realised that the voice inside me that I am calling my drive or my focus and which is used to having its own way, suddenly has an organised opposition. Actually, that's not true; when the voice suggests something, there isn't an organised response, more a wave of white noise that drowns it out saying 'it doesn't matter'. Occasionally the voice comes back with some financial or other imperative. But the wave is too strong and I end up lying on the grass with the dogs.*

So, the wave helped me to ground myself in now in 2009. But by 2010 the small things had started to reassert themselves. The palace reverted to being a shabby house. I became exercised by stuff at work that I knew didn't really matter. During my second cancer experience I wasn't in the least bit mindful. I focused on getting through, on recovering from the surgical shock, on being in control.

What struck me as most odd, when I engaged with the issue some months afterwards, was that the white patches were cancer related, yet I hadn't seen that I should adopt the mantra.

As I reflected, I realised that in 2009 there had been no conscious decision to ground myself in now. A white noise had developed, simply because of the gravity of the situation. I had to **do** something.

It may sound strange but almost as soon as I'd chosen my language in 2017 – **ground myself in now** – things became clearer for me. I understood that I had to have both feet solidly on (or in) what was happening now. On (or in) the room, or the train, or the field, or the pub I'm in. More important than my feet was, of course, my mind, which also had to be solidly in what was happening now, and not flitting about, casting forward and backward.

This took some thinking about. I started for the first time to think explicitly about how my mind works. I'd always tended to accept that what I experienced in my mind was actually me, how I am. I came to see that one of the things I've always prided myself on, probably that I've seen as being part of the essence of me, was just the sheer number of ideas that my mind generates.

Very few of these ideas ever get much further than being part of the buzz though. This, of course, is frustrating and allows me frequently to beat myself up for not having translated more of them into actions. When I really thought about it, I saw that the buzz of ideas was quite constant, quite tiring, and possibly not a good thing.

I also started to view the buzz as not actually being part of me. I've always been quite good at being on holiday, at not taking things with me; the buzz fades. Plus, the buzz slows and disappears when I'm tired. It was a critical moment when I realised that it didn't actually have to be like this; the buzz didn't have to be there constantly, I might even be better off without it. I could turn it off and run my life in a way where I set aside time to have ideas and time for my mind to be still.

Again I had help with this, it didn't just happen. Over the course of many months I engaged daily with Andy Puddicombe. I've never met Andy, he's the co-founder of the Headspace app and narrates most of their sessions. (Many) other apps are, of course, available, and I don't want this to sound like an advertorial. Headspace is just the app that Nick suggested I try. He later admitted that he hadn't actually even completed the ten free introductory sessions. He didn't tell me that until I'd become hooked.[21]

As we touched on when we talked about workaholism, I can be obsessive. I'm quite statistically driven and the app plays to that. The important thing, though, is simply that you find time to do something every day, or regularly enough to make a difference. Without that, nothing is going to change.

Wikipedia describes the app as *a digital health platform that provides guided meditation training for its users.* As one of those users, I'd describe it as the first of many things I've tried that's actually worked to regulate how I think and behave. Because I do it almost every day.

It genuinely feels that my mind has become a different place. A place with more space in it!

One of the key learnings I've got is very simple:

thinking is not a bad thing; the skill is to know when to engage in it.

In relation to the white patches, I said that the key was not to allow your mind to cast backwards or forwards. In Headspace language that's *choose when to engage in thinking.* Train the mind to see life as an endless series of individual moments, and be comfortable with the moment you're currently experiencing. Live in it. Be still in it. Experience it without serious thought. Think about when you choose to think.

For me it's a work in progress, but at least during the night I have overcome my tendency to indulge in negative thinking. It's as if I have developed a switch, as if I *can* control my mind. I tell myself that the night is a time for sleeping. The next stage (I think) is to create more of that stillness and control in interactions throughout the day.

I'm practising a few different techniques to use in these interactive situations. It's going to take time, but I'm certainly doing it with a very different mind-set. I'm also being kinder to myself, less judgemental of my mistakes. Previously, I'm not even sure that I understood what being kinder to myself might look like.

BEING ABLE TO NAME THINGS ALSO REALLY HELPS

In the same way that getting a diagnosis makes things easier, when I've found out that there's already a name for the things my brain does, it's just made everything much easier.

I've talked generically about the brain's tendency to cast forward and backwards, negatively. Here are two specific things my brain does that I now recognise and call out (as part of grounding myself in now):

Catastrophisation – involves thinking about the worst thing that could possibly happen. This sort of thinking, by the way, is genuinely part of a lawyer's training!

Selective abstraction – this happens when we are given a selection of material (for example feedback on something we've done) and choose to focus only on particular aspects of that material. For me, it's always the one or two negative feedback comments rather than the 23 positive ones.

In her excellent 2016 Commencement Speech at the University of Berkeley, Sheryl Sandberg[22] recently publicised a very simple set of ideas – the three Ps. They were originally the work of Martin Seligman. Sandberg talked about how helpful she had found these ideas in overcoming the sudden death of her husband a year earlier.

Personalisation happens when we believe that something happened *because* of us (or something we did) rather than simply happening *to us*. Sandberg had to accept that her husband didn't die because of anything that she did, that she couldn't have done anything to prevent his death. In the same vein, a client's decision to take the contract away from your firm was probably driven by budgetary necessity, not because of what you said in the meeting.

Pervasiveness is the feeling that because one thing is bad, everything is bad. In Sandberg's case, it's easy to see how her problems following her husband's sudden and unexpected death appeared pervasive. She talks about how her her friend, psychologist Adam Grant, got her to focus on the idea that her husband's collapse could have happened when he was driving her kids on the freeway. Tough love!

My sense is that I have normally been exercised by something that represents three or possibly 4% of the total. Which means that 96 or 97% is still working; still going fine. I've started to become better at focusing on the 96%. I have no idea where those numbers are coming from by the way.

Permanence is the third (and simplest) P. This is genuinely the advice that my Grandmother gave to me. Whenever I was worrying or sad, she had a simple phrase. It revolved around neither your greatest triumphs nor your greatest sadnesses lasting.

Sandberg said to the Berkeley class of 2016: *I wish I'd known about the 3Ps when I was your age.* I repeat these ideas because I've found them accessible and robust; they have really helped me to label and to combat negative thinking in the moment. If you're looking to ground yourself in now, to choose when you engage in thinking, feel free to use them yourself.

CHAPTER 5.

YOU'RE GOING
TO NEED A
TOOL BOX.
LET'S START
SIMPLE

If you're thinking about unleashing yourself, for a decade and a half I've used a straightforward, apparently transformational tool that may help you. It's known by the acronym **A-R-O** and was designed to help people in teams self-regulate and bring about changes in behaviour. It works because it's easily memorable, simple to use and positive – it focuses on what you can or might do, not on what's prohibited. A-R-O makes people think about conversations they could have, particularly when someone feels uncomfortable or psychologically unsafe.

In 2002, I was asked to explain to a group of equity traders the unforeseen consequences their behaviour was having, including legal risks for them. I didn't think that explaining the law would be enough. I spent time with them. They were adamant and kept repeating that they had no intention to offend. They were also surprised: how could people overhearing the way they treated *each other* have a problem, let alone complain about it?

Much may have changed, but we still use the tool every day and it could have been designed for a *#MeToo* world. Every day you move fluidly between three roles, you'll be an **Actor** and an **Observer** dozens, possibly hundreds of times each day. Hopefully you're a **Receiver** far less often.

You play the Actor role when you **do the thing** (say the words, send the email, smile at the person etc.) and the Observer role whenever you're **aware the thing's been done**. You either witnessed it first hand or you learnt about it later. So far, so simple and in the vast majority of workplace interactions, that's it – there are only Actors and Observers - there's no problem.

The Receiver role needs a little explanation: it doesn't mean that you are the intended or actual recipient of the thing (as the name might imply). Receiver is simply a neutral word A-R-O uses to describe anyone who's aware of the thing being done *and* who feels **uncomfortable** (perhaps **psychologically unsafe**) about it.

The tool relies on people playing each role mindfully and considerately. If we start with **Actors**, they need to show more self-awareness, more understanding of the impact they could be having on others. Recently I've started to think and talk about Actors needing to **leave more room**. Room for the other person's view, room to listen and room possibly to understand something of what's in the other person's mind.

In a *#MeToo* world Actors are certainly more aware of risk (and many are looking to put themselves in fewer risky situations). The challenge though is for Actors not to disengage, and to engage more mindfully, with greater understanding of their impact. This isn't easy, partly because different **people react differently** to the same stimuli. Sometimes the same person will react differently to how they have previously, because something's changed.

If A-R-O is going to work, Actors certainly need help from others. Often when I talk to real Actors (after an employment problem) they say they would like to have heard about the problem from a trusted peer or friend.

You may be thinking, this is all very well, but *what about the genuinely ill-intentioned Actors? They won't leave room or think about their impact.* I agree and what A-R-O says about the ill-intentioned is that there's no place for them in today's organisations. However, I set out in Chapter 1 my view that the vast majority of bullies are accidental, they're people who haven't thought about their impact, who haven't been approached by trusted peers to discuss the impact they may (unintentionally) be having.

It's also important that Actors don't simply make assumptions about how their colleagues will react. A story from New York in June 2014 illustrates the dangers of making assumptions and how everyone reacts differently. It happened during what New Yorkers insist on calling the *Soccer* World Cup. I was working with a group of commodities traders and had facilitated successful discussions with their colleagues in London and Singapore.

I'm pretty sure there were 18 in the room, all men. A very homogeneous looking group: predominantly thick set, 30-to 40-something, white, a lot of shaven heads. They worked together on a desk and bantered gently with each other.

In the London and Singapore sessions I'd done an exercise designed to show people that even their close colleagues see things differently. As I surveyed the group I hesitated, my mind full of assumptions. Surely it couldn't work – not with a group this similar.

I showed them a clip, in which Dave, a white, 30-something male, sits at his desk on a trading floor. He casually scans through images of a scantily clad female model (recently emailed to him by a colleague). Anyone on the floor can see what he's doing. Unfortunately for Dave (and the bank) so could anyone watching the lunchtime TV news. Because, apparently unbeknown to Dave, a spokesperson from the bank was being interviewed live and Dave's screen was clearly visible to the TV audience over the speaker's right shoulder.

I explained to the New Yorkers that the material on Dave's screen wasn't what would normally be termed pornographic, the model wasn't nude. These were shots you might see in a glamour magazine or possibly even glossy adverts. I also asked them to forget about the thing being live on TV. I just wanted them to concentrate on what they'd seen Dave do: casually opening, looking at and discarding the three images. In full view of everyone behind him.

Once they'd discussed the event together in small groups, I asked each of the 18 traders to decide if they *personally* were OK with what Dave had done. Would they be OK if someone did something similar in their workplace? I stressed that this wasn't about them giving a particular answer because they were in a diversity session. I repeated that the purpose of the exercise was to understand what they really felt.

What happened next was very normal in terms of my experience of running this sort of exercise, but seemed remarkable given the prejudices and stereotypes with which I'd approached the apparently homogeneous group. First, the group split in the way groups normally do – pretty evenly; half of them were OK with what Dave had done, half were not OK.

We went further. I offered eight options: from (1) *I am absolutely OK with this* to (8) *I am absolutely **not** OK with this.* When they raised their hands to show their position on the spectrum, each of the eight options was covered and no-one put their hand up alone. If there were 18 people in the room and at least two people chose each of the eight options, the group simply couldn't have displayed more diversity in its reaction to Dave's behaviour.

I understand that some of them may have been affected by being in a sensitivity session, thinking they had to answer in a particular way. But I'd been clear with them: I wanted to know how *they* felt. In the moments following the exercise I said nothing; if I'm honest I wasn't sure what to say. There was quiet in the room, no-one broke the silence with a light-hearted comment. The traders looked at each other and (I think) processed what they'd just seen. I think they were thinking about the assumptions they made every day, about what was OK in their group. I was certainly thinking about the assumptions I'd made.

As I said, *everyone reacts differently.* For me this sort of reaction (which I've seen repeated all over the world) characterises diversity at work. There are differences of gender, height, sexual orientation, ethnicity etc., and there is diversity of thought and reaction.

Getting back to the A-R-O tool, because everyone reacts differently, **Receivers** – anyone who feels uncomfortable – need to say something to someone about how they feel. Saying something may be slightly easier in a *#MeToo* world, but Receivers need to be assured and to trust that there's a path to follow and to feel comfortable looking for support. If they don't say anything, people will assume they're OK. If you feel uncomfortable about something and you do nothing, everyone I've encountered in every workplace I've worked knows that it's likely that the thing will continue and that you'll start to feel worse about it.

A-R-O suggests that there are two ways of saying something: *inside* or *outside the box. Inside* would normally be to someone else with whom the Receiver works directly. Route 1 is to the Actor, the person who made you feel uncomfortable. That may or may not be either easy or possible.

Route 2 is to someone else who you think can help you. That person becomes an Observer; if they weren't already aware that the thing has happened, they are now. There may also be other *inside the box* options: for example, employee resource groups or helplines offering support.

Route 3 is *outside the box*, to anyone in an HR or compliance type capacity to whom matters can be **escalated**. Whether your manager represents an *inside* or *outside the box* option has much to do with their style. A UK leader recently told me (after discussions with the people reporting to him following our session) that his goal was to be seen as an *inside the box* option. However laudable it may be to be seen as someone who keeps things informal, it's not always possible. I pointed out to him that sometimes the only possible reaction to behaviour is to take it *outside the box* (to complain formally or escalate).

Perhaps it's a question of the leader's style; it's about being more approachable and making clear that *wherever* possible you'll look for *inside the box* options and conversations. My strong preference certainly is for *inside the box* options. Because, in almost 30 years working with workplace problems, I have yet to see an *outside the box* approach result in a solution that everyone involved was happy with. I'm **not** saying that *inside the box* resolutions are either common or well received by everyone. This stuff is hard. My message is that we must all try harder if we're going to bring about resolution. I see too much of a tendency in today's workplaces to simply cede responsibility to others, normally HR.

Given the different legal and regulatory lenses that get applied to workplace behaviour, there's no simple rule about the best route for a Receiver to take. Much depends on the gravity of the thing that's happened, on who the Receiver is and many other variables including any applicable policies and laws. Suffice to say, the most dangerous answer is the one that feels the most normal: for the Receiver to do nothing.

On my iPad I have photos of my flip chart following literally hundreds of A-R-O discussions. Over the page is one from January 2019, a session I ran with six leaders in Baltimore. It's a bit of a mess, but the language the group generated in their discussion was extraordinary.

A-R-O FIGURE

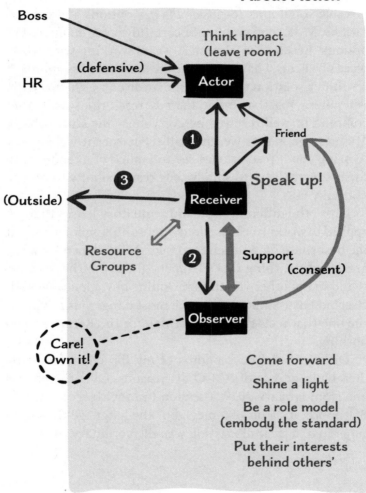

© Matt Dean 2019

Observers have a special role, a real opportunity to display their social sensitivity. My group in Baltimore came up with some incredible language to describe the Observer's role: it's for them to **come forward** and **shine a light** on what they find, I love that phrase. To be a **role model** and to **embody the standards**. Whose standards? Their own or the organisation's, perhaps wider society's? We'll return to this debate in Chapter 9 on Integrity. At its simplest, this is about Observers **caring** about the environment around them and **taking ownership**.

Often the Observer will be best placed to support the Receiver and this is an important part of their role: *were you OK with what just happened there?* The Receiver is very likely, by the way, to say that everything's fine. But just asking them shows that you care. Next time it happens, the Receiver might do something different. They may come and speak to you?

Observers are always going to be the largest group. If we can mobilise them, we can really impact workplaces. One result of *#MeToo* has certainly been that inactive observing is starting to be condemned and seen as enabling poor behaviour and abuse of power. Still many choose to do nothing, to carry on walking down the hall, *why would I get involved?* I hope you're starting to see why. Because your values tell you to. Because it's your workplace and you play a central role in creating the environment everyone works in. Because you can make a difference. *If not you, who? If not now, when?*

A COUPLE OF THOUGHTS ON HOW TO HAVE THESE CONVERSATIONS

Chapter 6 is all about making each conversation count. To get us in the mood for that, I'd like to share a few tips from my experience of talking to people about these sorts of conversations.

1. **Start with your objective in mind.** Before having the conversation focus on, possibly write down, exactly what you want to achieve. Hold it in your mind as you have the conversation. *I want him to know that I noticed. I want to let her know that I felt uncomfortable.* This could allow you to keep the conversation short and succinct.

2. Your tone is absolutely critical; keep your **tone** light and positive if you can. **Breathe!** This will become easier as and when conversations of this sort are normalised, as it becomes less unusual to talk about how we treat each other.

3. **Preparing for and handling emotions.** Given the subject matter, it's often inevitable that you (or the other person) will get emotional during the conversation. You can't not have the conversation because you're worried that someone may cry. I'm reminded of coaching a very senior man (who had a fierce reputation). After much soul searching he admitted that he was putting off an important feedback conversation in case the other person cried.

   I was taught (by a psychologist) that when someone starts to cry (or becomes angry), you simply need to create physical space for them to vent their emotion into. If you reach out to them physically or offer kindness, that will intensify things.

When emotion does arise, it helps to name it: anger, frustration, sadness, regret, etc. Also to empathise with it in a genuine manner, talk about similar situations when you have experienced that same emotion.

The safest thing to do if one of you becomes emotional may be to say, *let's break this now – we're going to get nowhere, let's come back to it.* And you must come back to it!

4. Always try **not** to assume that there's negative intent behind someone's actions. Remember the vast majority of people I've spoken to about the problems they've caused at work simply acted that way because they hadn't thought about the impact they were having. Not because they had evil intent.

5. When you're pointing out to someone that they've had a negative impact (on you or on someone else), it can calm the situation if you start by saying something like, *I know/I'm sure that wasn't what you meant to happen.* We'll return in Chapter 7 to the ideas of **impact** and **intent**.

6. Be prepared to come back to the subject at a later point. In fact, it might be wise to diarise it for seven or 14 days later, to set up a reminder that asks: *Should you check in with (X) and find out how they're feeling after your chat?* Be sure to jot down a note of the conversation you had. If you're anything like me, you'll have no recollection whatsoever of that conversation in a couple of weeks' time.[23]

CHAPTER 6.

MAKING EACH CONVERSATION COUNT

I think the first training session I ever ran was about negotiation skills for junior lawyers. I remember almost none of the content now. Apart from what BATNA stands for[24] and that you should give away what's cheap for you and valuable to the other side. However, something that either Fisher or Ury[25] said in an early example of the training video always stuck in my mind. People become Olympic swimmers because they focus on *the process* of swimming. They think about the angle at which their fingers hit the water and (I imagine) many more process points.

By contrast, the video continued, we spend a great deal of time negotiating in our personal and professional lives, yet we seldom, if ever, focus on the process. Many years later I met Dik Veenman. Dik's consultancy, the Right Conversation, took this idea to the next level. He was the first person I was aware of to sell to corporate clients the idea that they should train their people on how to have conversations.

Critically, anyone who Dik trained would be adept at recognising the constituent parts of each conversation and move to the next part more quickly: *What she is doing now is seeking to establish trust, what I should focus on now is ...* I had no hesitation then (and I am even clearer now) that this sort of approach would make all of us more effective in our professional and personal lives.

While writing this book I have also become aware of the absolutely fantastic work of Nancy Kline and the **Time to Think** platform.[26] Kline focuses on a framework in which we can think for ourselves, based on the theory that the quality of what we do depends on the quality of our thinking. Simple things matter.

Introducing structure to conversations is, quite simply, the way forward. Given that I'm suggesting we reach out to people outside our bubbles, I was transfixed when I first saw

Heineken's *#OpenYourWorld* campaign in May 2017. The adverts show what can happen when you bring together two people of opposing views. The viewer first sees short opening statements from both a trans person and someone who expresses transphobic views; an environmental activist and a climate change denier; a feminist and someone with conservative views on gender.

We see these unknowing, but potentially antagonistic partners (who are apparently unaware of the views of the person they're paired with) introduced in what look like experimental conditions. Each pair is given strict instructions on how they should interact; their interactions and conversations together are carefully structured. We see them following written instructions inviting them to pursue a joint task – assembling flat pack furniture to build what becomes clear is a bar.

They are then asked to describe what it is like to be them in five adjectives. Then, to name three things that they think the two of them have in common. The viewer watches that process. Once they are sat at the bar they've built with an open (and presumably chilled) Heineken in front of them, the partners are asked to view a short film: their opening statements.

The short videos are projected onto the wall behind the bar and the participants learn of their partner's views. The films were edited to show some obvious, initial shock, but when the participants being filmed were given the choice to leave or to sit down and discuss their differences (over a beer of course), they chose the latter. If you haven't had the chance to watch one of the ads, please go online and have a look. They're compelling viewing and show that you can bring about remarkable results by structuring conversations. The remarkable power of connection.

My premise is very simple: encouraging people effectively to structure their workplace conversations with people they wouldn't normally talk to will have significant consequences. There's an increasing realisation that conversations alone can change attitudes. I experienced in Jo Berry's exercise just how powerful simply being listened to can be and the transformational effects it can have.

It may be as simple as contracting with someone: *What do you want me to do? Just listen and say nothing, or perhaps you want me to try and suggest an answer.* It's also worth recognising that actually listening can do a great deal to transform what could be described as a low trust relationship. It's listening to someone that feeds their most human needs. It's been suggested that the brain may not be able to tell the difference between being listened to and being loved.

I'm always on the look-out for research in this area, and a very interesting study was recently written up.[27] The study concerned voting intentions and was conducted on doorsteps in Los Angeles. The top line finding was that political canvassers who talked to voters on their doorsteps for ten minutes about transgender issues markedly reduced prejudice against the trans population.

A ten-minute conversation was shown to bring about greater decreases in prejudice than the average American had experienced over the 14-year period between 1998 and 2012. The canvassers returned three months later and, apparently, the positive effect still persisted. Interestingly, transgender and non-transgender canvassers were apparently equally effective.

The canvassers were, of course, trained to approach the conversations in a particular, structured way. Breaking the doorstep conversations down, step-by-step, they looked like this:

(i) It was made clear to each voter that the transgender issue was potentially something they should have an opinion on. They were told that they may have to vote on whether to protect transgender people from discrimination.

(ii) Each voter was then asked about their views on recently passed legislation on the subject. Canvassers were specifically trained to listen and respond *non-judgementally*; in essence to *empathise* with whichever position the voter took.

(iii) Canvassers then showed the voter a balanced video in which proponents on both sides of the argument shared their views.

(iv) As the conversation continued, the voters were asked by the canvasser whether they may have experienced the sort of stigma or negative judgement that a transgender person might experience. At this point the canvassers were allowed to share examples from their own lives, where they themselves had experienced such stigma or negative treatment. The voters were invited to share their own experiences.

(v) After this, voters were asked again for their opinions and views on the recent legislation.

The research found that the second time they were asked, voters displayed significantly less prejudice.

The researchers, Broockman and Kalla, believe that the magic lies in mixing the two ideas: **active processing** and **analogic perspective taking**. Active processing is simply getting someone to engage with an issue in a thoughtful way. The researchers referenced Daniel Kahneman's famous divide between *thinking fast and slow*. In essence, if you get someone properly to think about a subject, to engage their rational thought processes, they will display less prejudice.

The second idea, analogic perspective taking is simply inviting someone to put themselves in someone else's shoes, getting them to think when they may have been in an analogous situation. Asking people about a specific time in which they have been judged is something I've done hundreds of times with groups in workplaces. I ask them to share confidentially, with a partner, their experiences of feeling different to others around them. In order to aid that process, I share a couple of stories from my own experience; stories in which I have experienced feelings of difference.

It's very much in line with my experience that to be effective and to get people to show less prejudice towards a group, you don't have to be someone who is in that minority group. In fact, I've always thought that it's easier for someone who's a member of the majority group to ask others in that majority group to think about how people in minority groups may feel.

SOCIAL ORGANISING IN THE WORKPLACE (AND THE ROLE OF TARGETED ONE-TO-ONE CONVERSATIONS)

The author Michael Gecan[28] is one of the principal exponents of social or community organising. I repeat this (quite lengthy) quote of his, simply because it captures so much of what I believed before I was introduced to social organising. The highlighting is mine.

*The trouble with many of us and with our culture as a whole, is that **we don't take time to 'relate'**, to connect publicly and formally but **meaningfully** with others. Instead we live in what Richard*

*Sennett called a **'tyranny of intimacy'** - presidents
pretending to share our pain or talk show hosts
prying into the most intimate corners of private
life. Or we feel a need to maintain **constant and
superficial contact with others**. We see and are
seen by others. We sit in meetings and conferences
and dinner sessions with scores and hundreds of
others. We **'touch base'** with others or **'make an
appearance'** or **'give brief remarks'**. We buy and
collect better tools - a tyranny of technology - to
stay in touch. But all **real life is meeting, not
meetings**. We don't take time to meet one to one
with others, to **hear their interests and dreams
and fears**, to understand why people do what they
do or don't do what they don't do.*

Now, let's consider the sections that I have highlighted and
break these down to see what Gecan is saying.

We don't take time to relate with others. This seems to
be the case even though it's become widely accepted since
the work of Deci and Ryan on self-determination theory in
the 1970s that relatedness is a fundamental human driver.
Despite this, we simply don't set aside the time to *meaningfully* relate with our peers (at least those with whom we
don't easily connect). This failure is maintained despite (or
perhaps because of) the constant and superficial contact
we have with others – on social media or in set piece team
meetings where we see and are seen by others.

We don't **hear their interests and dreams and fears**. We
don't understand why people do what they do. We don't ask
them about their interests, dreams and fears. If we did they
might tell us and what would we do with that information?
The answer is probably quite simple: we'd connect. We'd
make them feel more at home in this setting.

Gecan also said:

> *People who have ideas and drive are on every*
> *street, in every project, every workplace …*
> *Ready to be discovered.*

We can easily adapt the methodology of organising to the workplace and, in so doing, we can develop individual leaders around us. Remember the central definition of a leader in organising theory is:

> *Someone who accepts responsibility for enabling*
> *others to address their purpose.*

The social organising approach is one that first identifies those individuals who are potential leaders, who are directly affected by an issue and have a following. The organiser's role is to act as a catalyst. Once the organiser has identified those potential leaders of change, (s)he needs to meet with them and develop their understanding of:

1. ***The urgency, the importance of taking action.***
   (*If not you, who ? If not now, when?*)
   You typically do this by finding out how those people *really* feel about the subject; how closely it aligns with their values. Ideally, as an organiser, you're looking to generate in the people you want to become leaders an emotion that's akin to anger. It's this emotion that will translate into action from the chosen leader.

2. ***Their potential role in making something happen.***
   Often, the leader will not have thought about the idea that they can do something. They will have a limited view of their own potential influence. It's for

the organiser to make the leader see themselves as a person who can make something happen.

3. *How they can act effectively with others.*
What's incredibly important is to ensure that each discussion ends with a commitment to some form of effective action: *so what are you going to do to make this work?*

I can probably best illustrate these three preparatory ideas by reference to a real example of social organising in the workplace.[29]

Some time ago I was working in an international professional services firm; a partnership. There were a couple of partners whose behaviour was, pretty much, universally seen as representing an abuse of their position of power. There was no Weinsteining, nothing sexual, but bullying was the term used by many to describe their behaviour.

Partnerships are an interesting study in hierarchy, particularly when the transgressors have real power because they're high earners. There was a simple reason why the firm's (elected) senior management had not taken action against the transgressors, despite their reputation for transgression being well known: they billed too much.

In these circumstances, if we were going to bring about effective change, my job as an organiser was, first of all, to identify potential leaders: people who were directly affected by the behaviour and who had followers.

Those people didn't have to be other partners; I normally talk to people at all levels in a firm. I could have identified anyone who'd been on the receiving end of the problem behaviour and supported them to bring about change. However, in a conversation with me one of the partners, who worked closely with the transgressors, mentioned that their behaviour was something that made her feel angry. We'll call her Rachel. She and I took it from there.

Whoever the chosen leader of change is, however powerful or secure they appear on paper, they are going to be scared. Rachel certainly felt that she was putting her position at risk by saying anything. She was a junior equity partner.

What often works best in this situation is to help the person enunciate their values, to set out what's really important to them, and to ensure that they focus on the people who are being harmed by the behaviour at that moment. Rachel and I talked at length about how the behaviour offended her values and about a number of people, good people, who had left the team because of the transgressors. Also about people, again good people, currently in the firing line.

Before ending your first connection with the chosen leader of change, it's very important to agree what simple actions they will be able take before you next meet. In a number of situations, an organiser may have to meet more than once with the chosen leader of change. Or perhaps the organiser will take on the role of meeting with other suggested leaders, with a view to bringing about concerted action.

Rachel and I agreed that she was going to talk to a couple of her partners about the transgressors and about how they (what we might refer to as the non-transgressing group) could do something. I was, of course, on hand should the other partners want to discuss their role (as leaders of change).

The second critical feature of an approach based on organising is that any change will almost always **rely upon one-on-one, relational conversations**. When I first encountered the word relational, I was bothered by it. I distrusted it and thought it may be corporate speak. However, it describes exactly the sort of conversation we're looking for here, one that isn't transactional, one which doesn't relate simply to conducting business, but a conversation about the relationship we have that goes beyond the superficial.

Those relational conversations take place either between the organiser and the leader of change (Rachel in this case) or between the leader and someone they've chosen to speak to. In each conversation the objective is to give the chosen person the opportunity to explore and to genuinely understand how taking action will benefit them and those they care most about (in essence a repeat of my initial conversation with Rachel).

In situations of this type the benefit is often clear, particularly to the individuals on the receiving end of the transgressors' behaviour: their (working) lives will improve. It's sometimes less clear to the partners (and the firm's hierarchy) who need to envisage a new world in which the partnership may have to exist without the transgressors (and, more particularly, their fees). My experience is that simple **active processing**, thinking and talking about what that future may look like, helps enormously.

What Broockman and Kalla, the LA researchers, called **analogic perspective taking** can also help. Often, of course, the leader of change will have suffered at the hands of the transgressors. What was particularly interesting in the case I'm thinking about was that Rachel had not suffered, in fact many had imagined that she was going to become a transgressor herself, having been one of the transgressors' favourites.

A world in which the transgressors act as they always have and are successful with clients has become normal. What opportunities will open up if that behaviour changes, if the transgressors choose to move on? People often haven't done the visualising that these relational conversations can prompt. I think that in this situation those conversations were hugely important in bringing about a momentum for action. In this situation I watched as a number of people imagined how life could be without the transgressors.

The third feature of the approach is that change is created by individuals **acting together** to build wider **coalitions of support**. Those coalitions of support develop (ideally for themselves) a strategy for action. The best organisers are not going to dictate that strategy. I've consistently upheld that people never change because they're told to; they must see for themselves how they will benefit. An organiser acts with and not for people. Individual agency brings about change.

In Rachel's situation there were two central questions: (i) who would be the best person to have the conversation with each transgressor, and (ii) how many people (presently and previously employed) needed to be brought into the conversation before that happened?

There was an important question about the transgressors not feeling that their fates had been concluded by the simple volume of conversations. It was probably easier to say, *we've spoken to a few people and they have all felt the same*, than to say, *we've spoken to everyone who's worked with you for the last 11 years*. There was also a very clear sense that the transgressors should be approached on the basis that, *we're all clear that you don't intend to have this impact, but there is such a consistency of view developing that we feel we've got to raise it.*

Social organising is all about unleashing the power of people who care; it's a theory underpinned by what I've called in this book *individual unleashing*. The shape of change is very much in the hands of the people bringing it about. I very much believe that we'll see its power in the workplace over the next few years.

I'll conclude this section with some simple comments about social organising conversations in the workplace:

1. Organising conversations can involve external third-party organisers (whose role is to catalyse change) or workers (at any level) with a following operating as organisers. Anyone responsible for bringing about change in a workplace needs to think carefully about who they choose as an organiser. The selection of these people is critical to the success of any project.

2. These conversations aren't like normal conversations; the whole point of them is that they challenge what's seen as normal. They are also partly about agitation; they pick at a scab. A question that I often ask is, *what annoys you most about the firm?* After exploring the negative feelings people have, I will follow with something that sounds like, *what can you do about that?*

3. Organising conversations follow a simple methodology:
   - Start by being explicit, explain the purpose of meeting, what you're trying to achieve.

- Share your story – a personal story about you that explains why you're trying to effect change.
- *Tell me about you … What's important to you?* The key skill is to actually listen (I return to this below), to probe those things they may want to change.
- Remember to agitate – be explicit. You need to find out what makes them angry (if we're going to effect change); remember it's emotions that drive change.
- Explore how to change whatever makes them angry. Ask simple questions such as, *what needs to happen?*
- Agree simple actions to take, particularly for them. There may, of course, be people to whom the organiser should speak – with a view to setting up a coalition of support.

ACTUALLY LISTENING

There are whole books written about listening. There's a reason for that. If I was only allowed to focus on one thing, one skill in my quest to create kinder, fairer, more productive workplaces, it would be how we listen. In modern workplaces, normal for many of us is listening in the way that stressed problem-solvers listen, rather than as people who are curious and want to understand.

The most common explanation for this is time: *I simply haven't got time to listen to his problems.* Time pressure is, of course, the enemy of all people management. However, with listening, you can't not have enough time to listen. It's a question of mind-set, of how you choose to listen.

I was 14 or 15 when I worked for a few days in an old-fashioned café in a South coast resort during the summer holiday. I honestly don't think it was longer than that, however I learned many crucial life lessons there. One was how to butter bread properly. Another was the importance of **actually listening**. Today, professionally, I literally use this knowledge almost every day.

The proprietor was a magnificent Glaswegian woman whose name sadly evades me now, probably 40 years later. She had what you might call a remarkably strong accent. Had she appeared on today's BBC, her words would probably have been subtitled. But she taught me that it wasn't for her to change the way she talked; on the contrary, it was for me and everyone else she conversed with to actually listen.

What I learned was that when I focused on what she said, I could indeed understand her perfectly. I often use this idea in coaching and, of course, it's not just about accents. It's about people with different agendas and motivations too. I've come to use the word curious to describe the mind-set of an *actual listener*. Someone in the workplace organiser role absolutely has to be curious.

So much for the mind-set you need (**curiosity**), what about a bit of process? Three things:

1. *Trust your first question!*
Whenever you analyse someone's questioning and listening (and it's something I do very frequently) you notice that inexpert questioners/listeners tend to ask multiple questions. They appear not to trust the first question they ask, so they add in two or three sub-clauses or ideas. It's confusing; it blocks conversations; it allows someone to answer the question they think is the easiest and not the one you initially wanted to ask. Ask a simple, often open question (one which doesn't suggest its own answer, preferably starting with how or what), and then stop talking.

2. *Be comfortable with dead air.*

It frequently amazes me how frightened people asking questions seem to be of dead air. You're not on the radio, broadcasting to millions. You're talking to a colleague, it's just the two of you. Particularly if you're hoping that the other person will change their view in some way, they are going to have to do some thinking. So, leave space for them to do that. Be happy with silence.

If you're curious, if you want to hear what they think, don't introduce a new idea or fill the air with something that stops them thinking, just encourage them to say more. You can do that non-verbally or with my favourite directive,[30] a gentle *tell me ...*

3. *Use parenting to probe.*

It's a really simple technique, but it means you're actually listening. You use what they have just said as the parent of your next question. Refer to what they've just said and ask a simple how or what question. Or just *tell me more about that ...*

CHAPTER 7.

SIX MORE
PRACTICAL
TOOLS TO HELP
YOU MAKE
THIS CHANGE

If you want to make a difference in your own workplace, if you've accepted responsibility for enabling others at work to address their purpose, a few of the things I've talked about for the last decade and a half may help. They're ideas designed to allow you to shape your work environment, to help you be a more effective individual leader.

#1 YOUR SHADOW

This is just a straightforward visual that helps people focus on their influence at work. Whoever you are and whatever relationships you have with other people at work, I use the shadow to get you to focus on that influence and impact – to start to see how things may look to others. Obviously, you have a shadow outside work too, but let's start simple.

I'm conscious that the term shadow is regularly used in a number of different ways to talk about leadership. William Q. Judge wrote *The Leader's Shadow* as long ago as 1999.[31] He approached it from an academic background with the premise that leadership literature had become too focused on a leader's external influence. He wanted to explore the impact of the leader's character and addressed the negative connotation that Jung (1933) gave to the term shadow: the dark and hidden part of ourselves.[32]

My approach is very straightforward. When I talk to people about their shadow we look first at the externalities, the influence and impact they have on others, at how things may appear to those others. I don't restrict this discussion to the senior leaders in organisations because everyone has influence – whoever we are – so we all have a shadow. The visual we use is obviously a gross simplification. When you map actual relationships in organisations, the resulting images are called hairballs for good reason: they show the real complexity that exists in terms of inter-relationships.

YOUR INFLUENCE/YOUR SHADOW

©Matt Dean 2019

We've designed the visual to be simple and to get people to think about the relationships they have with the people around them. I think the first pictorial representation of a shadow I saw was a diagram of a stick man who stood at the apex of a uniform pyramid. There were two stick men on the second line, three or four on the next line, and so on for five or six straight rows. A uniform, geometric, monochrome pyramid (of stick men). My immediate reaction was that that was not how life was: life doesn't happen in monochrome straight lines.

In my discussions with leaders I started to draw collections of people of all colours and different sizes. I typically travelled with upwards of 15 different coloured markers. I started to get quite artistic in how I arranged the colours. The subject of the shadow was always drawn in blue.

You can't see that in the diagram we've reproduced here, nor that the others are other blues, greys, greens, pinks, yellows, reds, etc.

Over the years we've tried to move away from the basic stick person visual. A version of the visual that we use today is shown here in grayscale; it's supposed to be non-gendered.

The subject (you) is off to the side, not at the top. It's important to understand that your shadow, your impact and influence, is **not hierarchical**. Everyone has influence, and everyone is different, so influence is neither linear nor uniform. Your shadow will, by definition, include people in your team, people in other teams, peers, bosses, subordinates, basically everyone you interact with at work. They're all in your shadow because you influence all of them. If you have authority over others, they will be in your shadow. As will other people over whom you have no authority (or indeed who have authority over you).

Sometimes there's a discussion about whether people working for other firms are in your shadow. The answer to that is, of course, they can be. In today's workplaces your team may include contractors, vendors, and self-employed people; perhaps people on secondment from other companies.

Shadow denial is one of the most common reactions people have to the visual: *I don't have that much influence.* You hear this from the most junior to some really quite senior people. In my experience, everyone tends to think that they have less impact than they actually have. After showing them the visual and talking about it, they often realise that they have far more impact than they had originally envisaged.

Many, if not most, people (again, whatever their seniority) also automatically see themselves as being someone in another person's shadow. To use a powerful phrase given to me years ago, that's because we have *tunnel vision when it comes to ourselves*. We think first and foremost about how we're being treated, about what's happening to us. We also see everything in a way that suits us. Of course, you're in another person's shadow. In fact, you'll be in many peoples' shadows, but in order to focus on your impact you need to see yourself as the person in the top left corner.

#2 PLMS AND PNLMS

Of course, everyone understands that in real life and in real workplaces shadows don't actually look like that first visual. In real life, people clique. Each of us tends to listen to, socialise and spend time with, basically to care more about, the people we connect most easily with. I started using the simple phrases **PLM** (people like me) and **PNLM** (people not like me) many years before I was aware of anyone in corporate circles talking about **unconscious bias**.

Everything I've subsequently learned about affinity and confirmation bias supports that initial thinking. It's not my intention to delve too deeply into the area of bias in this book. It's been extensively written about and discussed elsewhere. However, the work of **Mahzarin Banaji** and others responsible for Project Implicit (and the Harvard IAT – Implicit Association Test) is widely respected and I would recommend everyone spends an hour or two working through a few tests.

In February 2016, a group of Swiss scientists[33] used the IAT in a study they published to show how we assess in milliseconds whether another human being is likeable or not; whether they should be in our in group. Connection is bound up (initially at least) with the limbic system, the automatic or subconscious mind.

Many of the people I work with seem unwilling to accept that their behaviour is guided by unconscious biases. Some seem to want to believe that they are cleverer than that, that they can somehow overcome or override these biases.

But my experience is that no-one disputes that they clique with PLMs. I've literally never encountered someone who denies that they do exactly that; that in reality their shadow looks more like this second representation.

YOUR INFLUENCE/YOUR SHADOW

©Matt Dean 2019

Remember, you're the person in the top left. Close to you there will be a group of people: they'll be the people you spend most of your time with, who you talk and listen to more, who you tend to have in your mind when you're making decisions. It's this visual that I want you to have in mind as you focus on what it might feel like to be one of the people in your shadow. In colour, the group nearest to you are various shades of blue or green. In my parlance they become your blue/green group.

What does it feel like to be in the lower groups, or that one person who doesn't seem to be connecting with anyone? Everyone I work with tends immediately to recognise that there's someone in their shadow playing the role of that lone person; not connecting and normally not behaving or performing as they could, or in the manner expected of them. We can introduce here the concept of the destructive cycle we looked at in Chapter 3.

People often say to me that that lone person could be quite happy; they may be someone who likes more autonomy, who likes to be left on their own. Of course they might. The challenge is to be clear that that is how they feel, that they are not feeling isolated or vulnerable. How do people who are feeling that way typically perform?

It doesn't have to be this way. That lone person isn't necessarily a poor performer; or a problem person. They're someone who could contribute more, but might not currently feel psychologically safe doing so. No-one's asking you to abandon or ignore your PLMs; that won't happen. This is more about focusing on and being more aware of the position of PNLMs.

In some ways the key themes of this book all centre on the PNLMs. The stifling power of normal is, in part, generated by you focusing predominantly on PLMs (the people in your bubble) and leaving PNLMs to fend for themselves. Remember, *life is about acting opposite to how you feel*. When you show humanity and empathy towards a PNLM, in a very small way you're doing what Jo Berry did when she showed her father's killer humanity. You don't have to start with someone who's harmed one of your close relatives. Just choose someone that your subconscious suggests you won't get on with.

Try to work through that initial feeling and reach out to them. It's not about needing to love them. It's more about adopting something like a **familial responsibility** toward them, toward everyone in your shadow. Each one of us is able to regulate our behaviour with people in a work context. Think about how you are with clients, bosses, or key stakeholders. You want to impress them; you think about how things might look from their perspective; you may actually listen to them.

You act like this with these important people, whatever your subconscious (or conscious) mind is telling you about whether you should like them. Why then can't we do the same with everyone we work with? Remember, all we're asking for is that we make those people feel psychologically safe, that they are listened to and get a turn in conversations.

How comfortable are you at focusing on some of these relationships with PNLMs? The simple message is that we *need* to get more comfortable. This is what Obama was talking about: *physically* (rather than digitally) reaching out to people not like you. In a workplace, it's far easier because there is, at least, a common connection – perhaps even a shared purpose.

PNLMs at work aren't like the people you may sit next to on the bus or tube/subway or whatever you call it in your country. So, let's start with the people at work. If it works with them, if we form some connection and make them feel safe and valued in some way, maybe the people on the tube/subway could come next?

#3 INTENT AND IMPACT

Before we leave the shadow, there's another idea that fits very well here. Let's assume that a behavioural problem has arisen in the shadow. A classic example would be the blue, top left person allocating a new piece of work to someone in the blue/green group (the group nearest them – with whom they connect more easily and often work) rather than to someone outside that group who would benefit greatly from the opportunity to do that work.

In almost all situations, when you approach the blue person and talk about what's happened, they'll offer an explanation for what they've done. It will be centred on what could broadly be called their **intent**: e.g. what they were planning, what they hoped would happen, maybe what happened the last time they did something similar. Or, perhaps, they didn't really focus on the situation, in which case they will tell you about their overall intent, that they are a good person, that they have a good record of successfully negotiating these issues, they deliver success and that they build high-performing teams.

YOUR INFLUENCE/YOUR SHADOW

©Matt Dean 2019

In the specific example of work allocation to the trusted PLM, the blue person (top left) will almost certainly talk about the time pressure they're under and the fact that they know how the person they've chosen will do the work – why would they take a risk? The performance of the team (or, perhaps, of individuals within the team) is very likely to form part of the way the blue person sees the situation and how (s)he justifies it. Because in today's workplaces (as we explored in Chapter 2) performance is typically treated as the Holy Grail.

What the blue person is doing is seeing the situation in a way that suits them, seeking to justify the thing that's happened **from their perspective**. This, again, is about us having *tunnel vision on ourselves*, not having the inclination or ability to see things from someone else's perspective.

At this point, let's be clear that it's the **impact** (normally the unintended impact) of the behaviour that's going to determine how people feel and whether we have a workplace problem. The other person doesn't see your intent, they just feel the impact of your action. They may well impute a negative intent to your action, an intent which in my experience is seldom there – at least consciously – and this can entrench a problem.

At its simplest the key driver of any employment problem is impact rather than intent. Occasionally, someone's intent can become relevant to the sanction; whether (or how much) someone gets into trouble for the behaviour.

Thinking about the **impact** of your actions on each person in your shadow can also be seen simply as **humanity**, being humane, kind, and benevolent. Having consideration for the impact you have on others is, perhaps, where humanity starts.

By the way, just because you're considerate and think about impact, doesn't mean that you'll get it right. Because the other person isn't you, because everyone is different. But adopting an impact mind-set, being more conscious of your impact, will help you to manage how you behave. I've come across numerous definitions of bullying in my work, perhaps my favourite, and the most simple, would be *not caring about the impact you have on others.*

And one final, important comment: being considerate about impact does not mean that you can't deliver difficult messages about someone's performance or behaviour. It just means you have to do that in a more considerate manner.

#4 BE CONSCIOUS OF BOTH YOUR AUTOMATIC AND COMPLEX DECISION MAKING

Something that may help you to be more considerate in your workplace is being more conscious of two levels of decision making. I'm always conscious that when I use this language I risk being accused of plagiarising the work of Daniel Kahneman[34] and his work *Thinking Fast and Slow.* My initial classification of workplace decision-making always had more to do with the impact of those decisions rather than how they are made: it's externalities again.

Everyday you'll make hundreds of **automatic, social decisions** (which I often refer to as **level 1**) and, possibly, depending on the sort of job you have, you might make one or more **complex decisions**. I see these more complex decisions as **level 2**, and I define them as being any decision that could impact upon someone's career. This will include obvious decisions like resourcing or work allocation, performance reviews, pay or promotion. Also less obvious decisions: whether to complain about someone's behaviour; whether to offer someone your support on a subject.

It's hardly a great stretch to suggest that we could all be more mindful of the impact our complex (level 2) decision-making will have. Because these decisions will, by definition, affect someone's career. The stretch is seeking to be more conscious of our automatic, social decision-making and the impact that these (level 1) decisions will have.

You get in a lift. Who do you smile at? Who do you say hello to? Who do you ask how they are? Your phone rings, it shows you who's phoning, do you let it go to voicemail or do you pick it up?[35] If you pick it up, what tone of voice do you use? You're going to get yourself a drink, do you offer to get someone else one? Perhaps you'll notice more of this sort of decision making the more successful you are at grounding yourself in now.

It's important to be more mindful of your automatic, social decisions because they have a great deal of impact. Particularly the more influence you have, but whoever you are, however shallow your shadow is, you have influence. Remember all of us shadow deny; we underestimate the influence we actually have. Level 1 interactions will affect someone's psychological safety, their confidence, whether they feel part of the in group, and, ultimately, those decisions will influence their performance.

This effect on performance means that there can be a clear link between your level 1 and level 2 decisions. Someone who feels confident in the group will perform better and it will be easier to allocate them work.

It can be very difficult to draw a clear boundary between the two levels of decision-making. Take a decision to involve yourself in an informal development conversation (a coaching type interaction) with a colleague: is that level 1 or 2? The answer probably depends on the formality of the conversation and, of course, your relationship with the person.

Perhaps it would be automatic if it was with a PLM, because that would feel more normal or natural.

Noticing and being more mindful of this level of your decision-making is an important part of the soft stuff. Remember that life is about acting opposite to how you feel, doing the thing that feels less natural. Maybe that's doing a bit of informal coaching with the PNLM.

#5 BRING YOUR WHOLE SELF TO WORK

We discussed this concept in Chapter 3. It isn't that difficult to see that being able to bring your whole self to work is an important part of feeling psychologically safe in a team. Recently, it was very clearly put to me by someone who said, *unless I do [bring my whole self to work] I'm just an actor. Only if I feel at home in a workplace can I fully invest in it.*

One story that's close to home concerns someone who worked with us at byrne·dean until she relocated to the US. Her name was Kalpana (which is pronounced with the second 'a' being soft – not the most difficult name to learn). When she came to work with us, Kalpana was about 15 years into her career. We were apparently the first place she'd worked where people said her name correctly. I asked her how that felt, people continuously getting her name wrong? It felt to me like an obvious example of not being allowed to bring your whole self to work. Kalpana said:

> *You're always on your guard, always checking yourself, and that's not going to help your performance, is it? Also, not saying anything unless what you're going to say is better than what everybody else is going to say. You want to stay beneath the radar, to get on with it and to work hard.*

All this from mispronouncing a name. I was struck by how easily she moved to performance and workplace behaviour. This conversation took place after a development meeting. In the meeting Kalpana's attitude had been described as deferential by one of our colleagues. I raised the word with her and her response still sticks in mind today:

I am deferential, I'm Asian,
I went to a comprehensive school
and I have a visual impairment.
Matt, I'm going to be deferential.

I hope that we worked well with what Kalpana brought to us; I saw her as deferential yet fierce! This stuff is never easy and it takes time for people to feel safe. I was in an internal meeting in which a colleague said to the group (which included Kalpana): *we're all white*. I remember that it felt positive when straight away, in the moment, Kalpana pointed out that, actually, we weren't all white.

She was sad to leave us, but there is a fantastic post-script to the tale. I talked to her recently about a project on Skype from Silicon Valley where she's in-house counsel for a tech company. She's now called Kal and she just felt somehow bigger, more confident, more sure of herself.

So far we've focused on how bringing your whole self to work affects productivity. In recent years, a key figure in the UK (and world) economy has pointed out that having one life and one set of rules can have another critical impact. Mark Carney is Governor of the Bank of England and he chairs the G20's Financial Stability Board.[36] He was the man charged with helping banking re-establish trust following the banking crisis of 2008–9.

In a key speech about inclusive capitalism in May 2014,[37] Carney talked about how our whole economic system depended upon trust in the financial system. He then stressed how important it was to rebuilding the foundations of trust in those financial institutions that individual bankers:

> ... *like all of us, need to avoid* **compartmentalisation,** *the division of our lives into different realms, each with its own set of rules. Home is distinct from work, ethics from law, the individual from the system.*

He was talking to all of us and he was saying that your home and work lives can't be separate. That the system requires individuals to bring themselves and their individual smell tests to work. If something feels wrong to you there's no question of applying a different test – a work test – to it. In my colleague Alison's memorable phrase, we all need to take their consciences up the escalator with us to work – whether we work in a bank, at Volkswagen or Cambridge Analytica. We'll return to this in Chapter 9.

#6 BE PROUD OF WHO YOU ARE, EVEN IF YOU'RE PRIVILEGED

As I've articulated, *unleashing the power of you* in the pages of this book, having pride in who you are has started to feel like an integral part of the mix. If you don't feel good about who you are and what you stand for, you'll inevitably diminish the power of what (or who) you can unleash. But how and where you let that pride guide you is crucial.

I write as reverberations from the Weinstein scandal continue and *#MeToo* is being used to document myriad transgressions, mostly by people who have characteristics in common with Weinstein. Let's be clear, it's mostly men; a lot of them educated, straight, white, married, non-disabled, etc.

People from our group have been in power for centuries. By implication we're responsible for the situation we find ourselves in today. Whether we're talking about the under-representation at the top table of people from outside our group or about the sort of egregious abuses of power that have been uncovered by *#MeToo*.

The focus is on us. How we react will set the tone for the next generation. We could become defensive, the angry white men that Michael Kimmel[38] has written about; fuelled by entitlement and anxious to protect our position in society. Many commentators have seen Trump's election as being in large part fuelled by a constituency of such men.

I'm acutely conscious of straying into gender politics and complex social history. Also, that it's so much easier for me to advocate generosity of spirit as a middle-aged, university educated, possibly a little overweight, straight, white bloke earning a good living. So, let me confine my message to workplaces and keep it straightforward and consistent: *we can choose the path of consideration and kindness.*

Let's not get caught up in any blame that we might feel is coming our way, or shame for things that we, or those in our number, have done. Those are negative, unhelpful emotions. Let's not lash out, harking back to a world in which we had the power. Let's understand that we are and have been privileged and let's use our power to create a new and exciting world, starting with our workplace.

We can't let the egregious behaviour of one (or some, or perhaps many) of our number come to represent what's typical. This an opportunity. In short, to show that we're better than that and we can do something about it. That feels to me like something we could be proud of.

What many of the men I've seen on social media are saying post-*#MeToo* is that we have it in our power to challenge abuses of power. To become the proactive, caring Observers that I advocated for in Chapter 5. This is about redefining what masculinity looks like in 2019 and beyond. To be a man could be to be brave and considerate, to display sensitivity and kindness, to understand that you have power and to use that power to create workplaces in which everyone feels safe and is listened to.

Part of the problem for my group is what's been described as the **good, bad paradigm** that developed as corporates increased their focus on diversity. This paradigm has marginalised men because it suggests that diversity and differences are good and that everything else is bad. People in my group will inevitably feel worn down by such thinking.

We need to abandon the paradigm. Any work being done to address inequality in workplaces needs to be focused on everyone feeling valued and on meeting people where they are. We're all unique and shaped by our personal experience of the world; we all have our own (very clear) pictures in our mind; we can call them biases and preferences. It is how it is.

As a discrimination lawyer, the key to my thinking in this area came when I saw that discrimination seldom, if ever, happens when I treat someone negatively because they're in a group that I don't like. It happens when I treat someone in a group that I like (a PLM) well, because I connect with them. Someone else sees that treatment and *feels* that it's better than the treatment they're getting. That person assumes that the better treatment they see the other receive relates to the other being in the group they are in.

Viewed like this, discrimination becomes more understandable, an extension of kindness and something fuelled by positive intention. And the solution is to extend that kindness beyond your immediate group.

In my experience, people accused of discrimination always deny it, forcibly. What they are denying, of course, is that they had any *intent* to discriminate. If we position discrimination as being far more understandable and that the solution is simply to extend your positive treatment of others (your humanity), perhaps we'll see progress.

What any focus on diversity and inclusion requires is that everyone feels **at home** and is valued for who they are and what they bring. An important part of this is simply recognising who and what we are, and that being the person we are may have given us some advantages (or disadvantages) which will affect how we operate and behave.

My middle son (who I perceive to enjoy particular privilege) regularly cajoles me to check my privilege. I think he means to be aware of it, to have it in mind. It's something we all need to do! How? Certainly, by thinking more carefully about how we are treated in comparison to others, asking those others how they feel and listening to anything they say. Also by recognising that if they don't say anything, it might not mean that everything is fine.

Having a clear sense of who you are and being proud of your heritage enables you more easily to imagine how someone would feel if their heritage, if some intrinsic part of them, seemed to be causing them to miss an opportunity or to be excluded somehow. Just like Broockman and Kalla, the LA researchers, in discussions about diversity I've always had the most success with people after I've made them focus on moments when they've felt different or excluded.

Kalpana is in my mind because I mentioned her in the last segment. Comparing what she and I perceive as normal has helped me to see just how privileged I am. The following two stories took place in similar environments, a decade or so apart. Kal's younger than me!

Kalpana's story
Between 1999 and 2001 Kalpana worked for a large law firm, spread over a number of sites, big enough to have

20 trainees, 17 of whom were white, and three of whom were from Asian backgrounds. Kalpana worked hard, she contributed a great deal during her two-year traineeship. As someone who has employed her and worked with her, I know just how much she offers. But, at the end of her training, she was one of three trainees not to be offered a job with the firm. She remembers being told that none of the opportunities seemed quite the right fit for her.

The other two not taken on were the two other Asian trainees.

Matt's story

Tim is someone I love. Since he retired as Senior Partner of his international law firm he's done some (fantastic) work with us, and for the last few years he and I have shared his Arsenal season tickets.

I met Tim in 1989 when he interviewed me for what were still called Articles of Clerkship. At that time, Tim ran the litigation department. I had recently returned from living in Singapore and Tim was interested whether Tiger was still the beer of choice. He was also interested in how I had come to be captain of college rugby in my first year. Was that due to circumstance (absolutely) or talent (much less so)?

I loved working for Tim and we worked well together. I messed up occasionally, but he overlooked what he referred to as my unforced errors. At the end of two years, there were three people who wanted a place in Tim's team. I don't think that the other two really stood a chance. I'd spent six months sharing an office with Tim and by that stage had been brought back to work with him from another department where I was supposed to be finishing my training because there was a surfeit of work, and the client had asked specifically whether I could return?

There are many ways to explain objectively what made me the best choice. The truth of it is simple. Tim and I made a personal connection, based in large part on our shared backgrounds and interests. Kalpana didn't get that opportunity.

It's a sloping playing field. At a conference recently I talked about how my youngest son had recently told me about a football game played on a sloping pitch in a strong wind. They were two-nil up at half time and lost three-two. Anyone who's played on a pitch like that (especially when the wind blows downhill) knows how difficult it is to score.

Despite what many people think, a focus on diversity and inclusion, a recognition that our biases and preferences are largely responsible for the make-up of today's boardrooms, and talk of quotas to break the glass ceiling – none of this requires us to be apologetic about who we are. The egregious behaviour of some (the Weinsteins) may lead some of us to question how we have behaved. Hopefully we will use the power we all have to bring about kinder, fairer, and more productive workplaces.

CHAPTER 8.

COMING TO YOUR PURPOSE (ALIGNING IT WITH 'THEIRS')

In Chapter 1 1 wrote:

Things 1 wish I'd known earlier in life: **when it comes to fulfilment, purpose is basically everything.**

If you're going to stop sleepwalking, you need to know what's important. That's as true for us as individuals as it is for the firms and organisations we work in. It's obvious to me, after years of what's probably best described as **career unfulfillment**, that purpose driven individuals need to put themselves in a setting that enables them to follow their purpose.

Somewhat ironically, the company where 1 first felt unfulfilled has recently been at the vanguard of the purpose movement. From 2010 the Unilever Sustainable Living Plan (USLP) has put purpose at the heart of Unilever's global business. Their purpose is to make sustainable living commonplace in people's homes.

The USLP has provided a blueprint for achieving the company's vision of growth while reducing its environmental footprint and increasing the positive social impact it has. Over the period of the USLP Unilever has averaged twice the rate of overall market growth and improved the bottom line. Their recently retired CEO Paul Polman has said things like:

I always thought that the role of business was to make a positive contribution to society. Otherwise why would it be there?

Polman is also clear that there is a business case to ending poverty. In a recent interview[39] he explained that if your brand mission is to solve a problem like open defacation (apparently 1.5 billion people do not have access to a toilet), the closer you get to solving the problem, the more opportunities there are for your business. Particularly, of course, if your brand is trusted and understood to be striving to improve conditions.

Had Polman been Unilever's CEO in the 1980s, I think my life would have been different. In 1986, on residential courses on Unilever's Management Development Scheme, I learned that a company existed to provide profits for its shareholders. I visualised retired vicars in seaside towns. I was socially aware and left-leaning. I'd made a decision to join a real company rather than succumb to the lure of the City. I felt let down, frustrated, listless.

Millennials were apparently not the first generation to look for more purpose in their work.

The mid 80s was, indeed, very much in the era that became known as Shareholder Value Capitalism. In a fascinating 2010 article,[40] Roger L Martin, Dean of the Rotman School of Management at the University of Toronto, sheds light on the moment when this second era of modern capitalism took hold. It began in 1976 with the publication of the most cited business article of all time, *Theory of the Firm* by Michael C Jensen and William H Meckling.[41]

The 1976 article accused managers of pursuing their own financial wellbeing over that of the owners and proposed shareholder value as the measure of good companies. The first era had, by the way, started in 1932 with the radical notion that professional managers should take over from owners. In his 2010 article, Martin was arguing that the third age should be about maximizing customer satisfaction. This third era has not happened quite as Martin predicted. In part because of the rise of purpose.

While writing this book I've got to know Geoff McDonald quite well, primarily in his role as a mental health advocate. Geoff's also a former Global VP in HR, Marketing, Communications, Sustainability and Water (that's some title) at Unilever, and was one of the key players, alongside Paul Polman, in putting purpose at the centre of their business.

In Geoff's simple phrase, we all understand that companies have to make a profit and grow, but that shouldn't be the reason they exist. The economist John Kay puts it well when he says:

> We must breathe to live but breathing is not the purpose of life. The purpose of a corporation is to produce goods and services to meet economic and social needs, to create satisfying and rewarding employment, to earn returns for its shareholders and other investors, and to make a positive contribution to the social and physical environment in which it operates.

Of course, Unilever's heritage does not tell a story of untrammelled profit maximization. You only need to visit Port Sunlight to understand that. The model village that surrounds the factory was described by the man who inspired it, William Lever, as an exercise in profit sharing. Today Port Sunlight consists of 900 Grade II listed buildings. Lever's aims are interesting to look at when viewed in the light of Polman's sustainable living plan. He set out to:

> Socialise and Christianise business relations and get back to that close family brotherhood that existed in the good old days of hand labour.

Since 2016, I've been loosely connected to the Blueprint for Better Business, a charity that exists to inspire and encourage companies to operate for a purpose that respects people and contributes to a better society. The charity is clear that organisational focus on purpose will deliver long-term sustainable performance. Much of their effort in the time I've been aligned to them has been on developing a body of research that confirms this empirically.

According to Blueprint the purpose of purpose is to:

- Inspire people [*I'd add for clarity 'within and outside the organisation'*] to contribute their personal energy to a collective venture.
- Reveal the human face of what the organisation is working to achieve.
- Ensure an authentic connection between what the organisation believes, says, means and does.
- Enable people to make practical choices about what they do day-to-day, using the purpose as a constant reference point.

Purpose certainly feels very much like the big new thing in leadership. In his TED talk *How to know your life purpose in 5 minutes*, Adam Leipzig, the CEO of Entertainment Media Partners, claims that Amazon lists 151,928 books on identifying purpose. He's exaggerating for effect, but undeniably there's an industry growing up.

In their HBR article in 2014, Nick Craig (President of the Authentic Leadership Institute) and Scott Snook (Senior Lecturer at Harvard Business School) commented that purpose was seen as being both the key to exceptional performance and a pathway to greater wellbeing. They mentioned that some doctors have even claimed that individuals with a clear purpose are more likely to be healthier.

There's an obvious danger that being more purposeful will come to be seen as a panacea for all ills. Geoff McDonald issues a stark warning to organisations who indulge in what he calls purpose washing; i.e. firms who adopt a sense of purpose as a marketing or reputation enhancing activity, but without properly living it within the organisation. Geoff's view is that you've got to make the firm's purpose drive performance.

Craig and Snook were also part of the team who worked with Unilever to place purpose at the centre of the business, and they described the process as painstaking. What's particularly interesting about their published work is that it seems to focus more on the need for individual leaders to develop a *personal* purpose than on the need for organisations to have a clear purpose or mission.

Craig and Snook centre on the benefit for the organisation of individual engagement.[42] The process they advocate involves leaders reflecting on their life experiences and sharing their life stories. As part of this process the leaders can prepare a sentence starting with: *my leadership purpose is ...* The participants can then identify their values and passions within that key sentence.

Craig, Snook and Geoff McDonald all stress that these clear statements of individual purpose are only one part of the story. The HR or human capital processes of the firm must also be adapted to reflect these purposes. Forms need to be redesigned, perhaps even with a picture of the individual leader and a statement of their purpose at the top of the development plan, or whatever the form is. This is what's actually going to change the conversations that make up the firm's culture.

Each leader would need their own personal development plan. What exactly will be happening in 12 months, in six months? What concrete action are you going to take today to start achieving your purpose? Who is going to support and help you achieve the plan? You won't do it on your own, and this isn't just about others in the organisation – some of the relationships will be external, such as friends and family.

Of course, there's a risk that, having established their leadership purpose, an individual leader may very well question whether they can actually achieve it in their current place of employment. Firms that pay big money to consultants to help their top people find their purpose run a risk. At the end of this chapter I return to what to do if you find yourself in the wrong setting.

CAN YOU KNOW YOUR LIFE PURPOSE IN FIVE MINUTES?

I've seen individual purpose defined in a number of ways. At its simplest, it's your reason for getting up in the morning. More complex would be: *your purpose is determined by leveraging your skills and aligning your needs, values and aspirations with the impact you want to have on the world.*[43] I think that we get up in the morning for complex reasons and that the second definition is maybe a little too complex to remember. That said, I obviously applaud the focus on impact and it covers what your drivers are and what you're good at.

Let's start where I started – with something that I've since decided doesn't work! Adam Leipzig's TED talk has, after all, had over 13 million hits.[44] Blueprint used his framework as a start point in their immersion course. For me it's just that: a start point. Let's be honest: you're not going to come up with anything as important as your life purpose in five minutes.

The important thing is that you understand why purpose is important and, hopefully, that you will want to start your own long, hard slog towards putting yours into action. Energy and motivation will flow from you spending time examining a question that sounds like *what's it all about?* In an ideal world you'll come up with a simple, memorable phrase that can ignite your passions, is aspirational yet achievable, challenging and personally fulfilling.

Here's Leipzig's simple framework, with a bit of commentary from me.

1. **Who are you?** This isn't just your name! The more time you give to this question the better. The first time I did this exercise properly we were in pairs. I learnt a massive amount about my partner. He started with his religion. He told me about the (manufacturing) businesses that he had set up across the world and how he wanted to find out if purpose could help them.

   I think I started with a list of my roles: husband, father, son, brother, business owner, moving on to former lawyer, subject matter expert, etc. What's become clear to me over time is that your purpose needs to come from **the essence** of you.

   I now combine the question with a fantastic exercise I learnt from Jorge Farias, an inspirational coach and trainer, and the man who first helped me to understand inclusion properly.[45] Jorge taught me to get people to select just three words that capture **their essence**. The need to choose just three is important because there's no room for anything spare.

   My three[46] start with a word that means someone who just can't accept the status quo. If I'm being kind (to myself) I think the word is something like **moderniser**, but it could equally be something like **tinkerer**.[47] Then I'm a hopeless **liberal**. Liberal is an interesting word; for me it encompasses left-leaning tendencies and possibly radicalism. However, and interestingly, given the book I'm writing, its dictionary definition suggests that as a liberal I'm willing to respect behaviour and opinions different to mine. Maybe I need to rethink? I think the third intrinsic part of me is my **emotional** nature; I cry a lot and struggle to rein in my emotions. Anyone who's ever played (or even watched) sport with me or watched me speak publicly about any potentially emotional topic will get this.

In addition to your three words, there will be your stories. During training as a social organiser you focus on the stories about change you might tell others to gain their trust and to elicit their stories. I very quickly told a story about the first time I appeared in court. It was a discrimination case. There were nine of us in suits on the left of the tribunal room. I'd done hundreds of hours of preparation, I knew the facts inside out, and the law. A good number of the other eight had probably spent almost as many hours as me. On the right was a 19-year-old black girl from South London I'll call Jade (with her Mum). Jade managed about 25 minutes before she walked out.

I clearly remember watching her Mum very closely as the Judge (actually then called a Chair, but that's boring detail) explained that he had no option but to find against Jade. I was aware of the emotions around me, on the left-hand side of that room, and of those on the other side. I knew at that moment that something had to change.

Stories like that (and your three words) will very quickly take you to your values. Let's not make this any more complex than it needs to be: your values are very simply the things that are really important to you.

2. **What do you *love to* do?** Leipzig's second question is not simply *what do you do?* He focuses on the bit you love. I think that is because your purpose needs to motivate and inspire you, you need to love achieving it. Whenever I ask anyone to focus on this question, someone inevitably asks *do you mean at work?* I don't think you should necessarily start with (or confine yourself to) the bit of your life that's currently remunerative or productive.

Leipzig I think is talking predominantly to people like me, working in the knowledge economy or in jobs with the potential to fulfil. He talks about happening across his formulation for discovering your purpose at an Ivy League class reunion.

But, as technology starts to reduce the number and types of jobs available, perhaps we have to think in terms of one life, one purpose. Maybe you can make your hobby your purpose? I increasingly encounter people doing just that. When I did Leipzig's exercise properly[48] I came up with a list of seven things I loved doing; they've been helpful for me. I reproduce them here as an example, and so that you can see how such a list could possibly help in establishing a purpose. Or maybe not!

I love:
- *getting into my comfortable bed, tired and fulfilled because I have worked hard*
- *being with people I love; laughing and drinking beer*
- *ideas – simplifying them and coming up with ways of explaining things*
- *people listening to me, being entertained, and helping them see things differently*
- *cinemas, beaches, anthemic music, and football crowds on a Saturday afternoon; watching the match (any match!)*
- *drinking (decaf – which tells its own story) coffee, eating chocolate, and having crisps at lunchtime.*

If you're struggling to make sense of this, Leipzig helpfully suggests a supplementary question: *What are you uniquely qualified to do for people right now?* It's worth a try. Once upon a time though I was probably uniquely qualified in the UK to train people about the fundamentals of data protection law, but I think I would have struggled with that as part of my purpose.

My proposed solution for this question would be along the lines of: *what do you love to do that could provide for your material needs?* For many of us that will translate as *what will people pay you to do?* Some may have no need of money.

3. **Who do you do it for?** It's at Question 3 that I diverge from Adam Leipzig. His intention is to get you to identify the people to whom you provide what it is you love to do. He wants you to focus on the impact you have on them. Just look at the next two questions: **4. What do those people need?** and **5. What changes as a result?** He wants you to be able to get to a place where you can say: *I exist to do [this thing] for [these people] – and it creates [this change].* It may work for some of you, it didn't for me.

For me, the question, *who do you do it for?* took me to the various populations to whom I'm accountable: me, my wife, my boys, other people I love – family, friends, and colleagues, and everyone I touch in my work. We'll come back to something like this list in Chapter 9 – because, for me, recognising who you are accountable to is the centrepiece of acting with integrity.

The only thing I could see that all of those people *needed* (and this was a stretch) was for me to be true to myself, to enjoy what I do and to derive meaning from it. In its own way, this realisation was useful to me, particularly given the (challenged) mental state I was in when I first discovered it. But it didn't provide a life purpose or a simple, memorable phrase that would be of any use day-to-day.

Luckily though, I had the conversation I describe in Real Time Intervention 3.

PERHAPS, IRONICALLY, THE BLOKE I MET ON MY FIRST DAY OF REAL WORK HAS AN ANSWER

I met Andy Bird on my very first day at Unilever. We've remained firm friends ever since. In my mind, everything Andy does, he does supremely well. Perhaps, surprisingly for such an omnitalent, I genuinely can't imagine anyone not thinking that he's a lovely bloke.

He stayed at Unilever much longer than me and then co-founded Brand Learning, a very successful company that's now part of Accenture. He works as a coach and recently wrote an excellent book called *The Inspired Leader*, in which he's nailed quite a bit of the soft stuff. Andy was nice enough to write about me in his book, so I'm returning the favour!

Summarising Andy's book in a sentence, he says that inspired leadership comes at the intersection of your **values**, your **passions** and your **strengths**. Exploring *who you are* and *what you love to do* should allow you to identify your values and your passions. But the new idea here is the focus on what you're really good at.

I absolutely welcome the focus on finding our strengths that's become an important part of leadership in recent years. We don't focus half enough on our strengths! Far too often we try to fix our perceived weaknesses (or those of others around us). However, many of us don't see what we're good at. There may be a role for someone to help you with this?

So, the formulation becomes three (simple) questions:

1. **What's the essence of me?** (Which, if you answer properly, will elicit your values.)
2. **What do I really love to do** [possibly add **'that could provide for my material needs'**]?
3. **What are my strengths?**

And from there can come one sentence: *my individual purpose is to ...*

It will take time and you'll have to work at it. But remember, unless you can remember it and repeat it to yourself easily, there's little point in having it. Because you won't use it or hold yourself to it. It'll just sit on you desk and get covered in other papers.

HOLDING YOURSELF TO IT, KEEPING YOUR PURPOSE FRONT OF MIND

Creating it is only the first (and probably easiest) step. How do you keep the idea of it front of mind and guiding you day-to-day? How do you make use of it?

It probably makes sense to set yourself some longer term (three to five year) goals, but work back from there. What are things going to look like in 12 months or six months? A period that is immediate. Set yourself three, straightforward short-term goals. These will act as a bridge between where you are now and where you want to be. Every day or every week, make sure that you're doing something towards each one of them.

After two or three months, you will need to look and see how far you have got with the three, and assess whether they're the right three or not. You can pivot (which is the modern way of saying change direction), always having your long-term plan in mind.

Actually, that's all true. What I've just written is a great process. But if you want this to stand a chance, the critical thing is to change what you do every single day. Nothing is going to happen unless you think about your purpose **every day**. This has occurred to me very lately. The reason why I've been experiencing some limited success with this stuff recently is so very simple; it's because I'm setting aside time every day to think.

I'm not thinking specifically about my purpose, but I have a purpose and I'm spending 20 minutes every day being mindful. How you think, being mindful and having a purpose are all part of the same whole. I have a purpose and I'm being more mindful. I have a plan and I'm not sleep-walking. The daily practice thing is the key to all this.

AND WHAT ABOUT CONGRUENCE?

Of course, for many people there will be that sense that they won't be able to achieve their purpose in the setting, the firm or the organisation they're currently in. There are probably three options.

1. **Move to a new setting**

   Many organisations talk about their purpose, their societal value. You will need to assess whether you think there's real commitment or whether they are engaging in purpose washing. This is the sort of thing that you can ask about in the recruitment/engagement process; it's not easy to bluff purpose. More importantly you'll learn whether the individual you've asked genuinely believes the organisation has a purpose (and/or has one themselves).

2. **Volunteer**

   I tried for many years to satisfy a desire for meaning by way of voluntary work at evenings and weekends. This was partially fulfilling and can be a good option. Also, it certainly provided an opportunity to develop my leadership/connections and was perceived as a good thing by the firm who paid me. I did this before family responsibilities kicked in, reducing the energy I could invest. It felt easier then.

3. **Change the setting you're in**

Drawing from the contents of the whole book, if you want to give this a try I'd suggest the following approach:
- Clarify your individual purpose.
- Focus on what I've called congruence, how easily (or not) you can achieve your purpose in your current setting.
- Have a good hard look at what's in front of you and, if you want to stay and think it's worth a go:
  o consider what you think the organisation's purpose should be;
  o come up with a compelling personal story that explains why you want to effect change;
  o choose people with a following in your organisation;
  o start a conversation with those people about organisational purpose; engage with the leaders you've chosen using the organising methodology I've set out earlier;
  o focus on simple, day-to-day actions; they are what brings about real change (and potentially on building a coalition of support around organisational purpose).

Good luck with that!

REAL-TIME
INTERVENTION 3

MORE BEARDY GURU
THAN CITY BOY

So I'd worked through Leipzig's five questions;[49] I thought that I'd done the hard work on identifying my purpose. I was initially pleased with the results. I'd got it on to one page, which appealed to my innate sense of neatness and presentation. The process had given me some clear and useful insights.

I'd come up with the list of what I love to do. The more I reflected on the whole getting into bed tired thing, the more bothered I became about how that was just because I was a sad workaholic. More importantly, the process hadn't produced a simple phrase or idea; something I could actually use. Probably as a result, I hadn't actually done anything with it. The one page sat on my desk and was having no impact on my life.

Also, and with hindsight, I hadn't started any daily practice at this stage. These were all ideas that could be helpful if I wanted to use them. Fundamentally though, this sort of thing can only be helpful if it's so simple that you can bring it to mind easily and check how you're doing. At that moment though, in May 2017, I'd concluded that the process was more complex than Leipzig made out.

As I was researching *purpose* for Chapter 8, I read quite a bit of new material, much of which struck me. A fantastic phrase of Oliver Wendell Holmes Sr, the Victorian physician, poet, and polymath, based in Boston, sat with me:

Most of us go to our graves with our music still inside us, unplayed.

Of course, that's what I'm afraid of. I wonder if it's what we're all afraid of, or if that's my cancers talking.

The words probably had more impact because a year or so before one of my colleagues, Alison, sent me a hugely powerful video clip. The words of Alan Watts, a British philosopher best known as an interpreter of Eastern philosophy for a Western audience, connected to images on *Vimeo*.[50] It said a great deal to me. Particularly, I think, because I knew that I had had my own epiphany, in his words I'd *woken up one day around 40 years old*. I was actually 44 when I had my first cancer, but I hadn't made the transition Watts talks about; I'd not made the dance the whole point of dancing.

Please look at the clip, but I reproduce some of Watts' words here:

> *The existence, the physical universe is basically playful ... it doesn't have a destination that it ought to arrive at ... it is best understood by analogy with music. Why? Music differs from, say travel.*
>
> *When you travel, you are trying to get somewhere. In music, though, one doesn't make the end of the composition the point ... If that was so, the best conductors would be those who played fastest ... People would go to concerts just to hear one cracking chord!! Because that's the end.*
>
> *Same way with dancing. You don't aim at a particular spot in the room ...* **The whole point of dancing is the dance.** [My emphasis]
>
> *We have a system of schooling which gives a completely different impression. It's all graded and what we do is put the child into the corridor of the grade system with a kind of, 'come on kitty, kitty' ... And when you're through with graduate school, you go out to join the world.*
>
> *Then you get into some racket where you're selling insurance and they've got that quota to make, and you're going to make that.*

*And all the time, the thing is coming … That great
'thing'. The success you're working for.*

    *Then when you wake up one day about 40 years
old and you say: My God, I've arrived, I'm there.*
[Laughs] *And you don't feel very different from
how you've always felt.*

    *And the thing was to get to that end. Success, or
whatever it is. Or maybe heaven after you're dead?
But, we missed the point the whole way along.*

    *It was a musical thing and you were supposed to
sing or to dance while the music was being played.*

Just returning to the research I did on that Friday afternoon, my notes contained the following sentence:

*Your purpose springs from you – the essence of
who you are. Look into your childhood, mine your
life story for common threads. Don't do the exercise
on your own.*

The very next morning was a Saturday. I was in a coffee shop and it was sunny. My dancer was dancing. He was in his last year of school and I regularly took him to rehearsals. I was texting a friend, Doug, who I've known for over 30 years. We met at college; we've grown up together: from our early years establishing careers, (re)finding partners, weddings, young children, cricket, football, politics, older children, always meeting for drinks, always talking and listening. Good times.

    *M: Do you want to come to the Man U game
        tomorrow? Just realised I've got the tickets.*
    *D: To witness the funeral rites? Sorry Matt can't.
        How are you?*

How was I? [*It's important to remember that, while I'm calling this Real Time Intervention 3, it actually happened before Real Time Intervention 2. I hadn't sought professional help yet.*] How had I been since the white patches on the tongue? Not great if I'm honest. I thought, possibly, low-level depression; I certainly knew I was having a negative impact on others. I had, at least, arranged a psychiatric review with one of the doctors at the Marsden. My response was:

I'm ok thanks. It's been pretty up and down, but in the big scheme of things, what's the point of being down?

Doug phoned and we talked. He was lovely and I felt blessed to have supportive friends. Fifteen minutes later I noticed that I had another text from him.

I have a suggestion to make if you have time …?

Of course I had time. I was sitting in a sunny coffee shop writing a book! But I think the point is, make that time. **Actually listen**.

What followed was extraordinary. It now feels like I'd been waiting for someone to tell me what to do! Doug analysed in a couple of sentences what he thought had been going on for me: in his mind I'm an alpha male bloke with a string of anxieties and a lot of anger – he mentioned the way I've always played sport. He played most of it with me.

His analysis was that cancer has taken away my ability to be that alpha male. He suspected that it had challenged my ego. But I'd come through it – twice now. He talked about how important he could see my trip to New York (after the operation) last year had been, and how important to me being fêted is.

He thought that that ability to be fêted had all been threatened again by this latest experience. His view was that the white patches would have hit anyone hard. But in Doug's mind, I already knew what the answer was – he said I'd told him the answer while we were talking earlier that morning. It's all about living in now; making the most of what you've got, not about how to continue making a good living.

Doug told me about an inspirational friend of his who was living with cancer and who had, very convincingly, reinvented her life. I wrote down: *Diet, blankets on the sofa, time with friends etc.* Doug's advice was simple. Simplify your life. Sell the house, sell the business. Get something small. Walk the dogs and take it a bit easy.

Then (he said and) I wrote: *Look at what you did when you were first ill; homespun truths from Matt Dean. You like that hippy shit. You don't give it a chance.*

My notes continued: *Recalibrate! Be the beardy guru not the City boy. I know that's always been a tension in you.*

Would it have been more powerful to reproduce my actual notes here? Would it be more important to talk about how Doug has always followed a path that is more righteous than mine, and how difficult he's found that path too? I don't know. I'm just talking about how I felt on that morning, while my dancer was dancing.

Doug talked about my death bed and how I would feel. We'd talked earlier about us both being stalked by mortality; me more than him, but … Then he said the thing that just made me stop and which I knew – in that moment – was going to have a massive impact. *I'm not an oncologist but the 110 mph way that you live your life; it's not the best way for a cancer sufferer to live their life. And you do live your life like that, don't deny it.*

Just so you know, it was those words that made me start with the daily practice when Nick suggested it. Right there. That's it.

Talking a few months later to my wife, she was shocked that these words could have had any impact on me at all. To her, I think they were unremarkable words. She knew this. She was clear that I knew this. Perhaps everybody who knows me/knows us, maybe they all knew this, maybe they even say it to their partner frequently. Possibly they'd even said it to me (but in a way that I didn't hear)?

Why did those words, in that moment, in the sunshine in the café, why did they make me cry? Why did I know then that I was going to do something about my 110 mph lifestyle?

Because I prize Doug's judgement? I don't think I do particularly. At least not more than anyone else's! Because I had spent a long time lost and knowing that I had to find a solution. Or simply because I was ready to hear them in that moment and actually listening.

The work I'd done the day before, the interplay of Wendell Holmes' words with those of Alan Watts. I think I may have been preparing to take control. Anyway, literally straight away, I knew that I had to change the pace at which I moved. And my purpose came very shortly after.

Doug had commented on the tension in me that he'd been conscious of, that I had not given the beardy guru a proper try, and that I wanted to be that person. And it's clear to me from the work that I've done on this book (and elsewhere), in the words of Adam Leipzig, what it feels like I'm uniquely placed to do. My purpose is to be more of a beardy guru than a City boy. I want to dedicate myself to helping people see and shape the impact they have.

My purpose is actually helping people see and shape their impact. The three words **more beardy guru** capture the essence of it for me. These three words create a simple, usable phrase that I understand and that can guide me; that takes me straight back to that morning my dancer was dancing.

A POSTSCRIPT?

There are a few people in my life who go back further than Doug. Chris and I met when I was 11 and in my first year of secondary school. He was my best man and continues to be a thoughtful confidant. He listened carefully to me as I recounted the conversation with Doug. Then he said: *You can't just switch that other side off, it's why you've achieved what you've achieved.*

I was initially a little deflated. I had bought into my new purpose and wanted everyone to love it as much as I did. But, of course, Chris was right. It's going to be me driving this new purpose; in fact shortening it to *more beardy guru* may allow me to be myself – the driven person that everyone has come to expect. Just doing *more* to help people see and shape their impact. More of what I would see as the natural work of a guru!

CHAPTER 9.

INTEGRITY IS THE HOW; BUT WHAT ACTUALLY IS IT?

Literally the day before I sent the final manuscript of the book off to the publishers, I sat down to rewrite this chapter. The chapter I had was OK, but it was too complex. Integrity needs to be simple. Having chosen the path you want to follow, you need a mechanism to guide you along the path. For me that was going to be integrity; which means the straightforward idea of always being true to yourself (and to your new found purpose).

In Chapter 4 I made the point that many people struggle to define integrity. They will mumble something about, *doing the right thing* to which they may add, *when no-one is looking*. Before we go any further I need to get one, I think quite important, thing off my chest: there is never going to be just one right thing to do, one simple choice that will be correct. There will always be any number of choices. Surely the stock phrase could be *doing **a** right thing?*

The idea of acting in a way you deem correct when you're the only person who knows about your choice(s) is certainly a critical part of the equation. Integrity is first and foremost about not letting yourself down. I think the reason why many people struggle to define integrity is simple: they haven't done the preliminary work on their values, on understanding what's important to them, and how they want to live their life. They've been sleepwalking. Once you've done that work, integrity becomes a far easier thing to understand.

Whenever anyone tells me, integrity is about doing the right thing, I make a point of asking: *Whose right thing? Yours? Your employer's? Society's?* This gets people thinking. When choosing how to behave in many scenarios, there are likely to be a number of potentially competing rules at play. Can you act with integrity, but, for example, break society's laws, your employer's code of conduct, or go against another person's moral code or values?

Of course you can.

Nelson Mandela was seen by many as a terrorist when he took action against apartheid South Africa. He famously said:

When a man is denied the right to live the life
he believes in, he has no choice but to become
an outlaw.

I think about these words every time I talk to a whistle-blower or contemplate the idea of whistleblowing; of reporting potential misconduct amongst your colleagues. Whistleblowers, in common with outlaws, stand outside the group.

Mention of whistleblowing brings us back to the idea of avoiding compartmentalisation that we touched on in Chapter 7. Of the need to carry our personal values, our personal smell tests, with us at work at all times. The motivation to act with integrity comes directly from those values, and possibly from our purpose.

I've found the most powerful definition of (or, more correctly comment on) integrity from the philosopher, Albert Camus. By the way, philosophy for me literally started with Camus, in a French A Level classroom. Camus' suitably anarchic suggestion was that:

Integrity has no need of rules.

When we act with integrity, we hold ourselves accountable. We regulate our own behaviour. We set the rules.

I think that Camus may have had quite a bit to say about the financial crisis of 2008. A big part of the learning following that crisis was that the regulators' rulebooks had become too dense, too prescriptive; there were just too many rules. So people focused far more on the detail of the rules themselves, on whether the rules specifically prohibited the action they planned. They relied far less on their own consciences and smell tests. We all need to understand that.

Part of my mission is reconnecting people with their consciences and ensuring they're more conscious, more thoughtful about more of their decision making. I've talked in Chapter 6 about level 1, automatic social decision making. It feels to me that in the aftermath of *#MeToo* there's a moment of reflection for all of us. Similar to what was required of bankers post-2008.

We need to reflect on how we behave; not just when we're making level 2 decisions that affect people's careers. We need to reflect on how we behave with the people around us, our friends, and our colleagues at work. Employers and regulators have always created far more detailed codes and rulebooks about how to conduct the detail of the jobs we do than about how to behave with each other. As the ground has shifted post *#MeToo*, many employers have considered adding that detail.

In June 2018, Netflix, a company I recall frequently lauded as a thought leader in the HR world, was reported[51] as having introduced workplace rules concerning how long you could look at a co-worker and how often you could ask for their telephone number. Online reaction to these reports was generally negative. Every time I've discussed the idea of a more detailed set of workplace behaviour rules with people in workplaces, I've had similarly negative reactions.

In March 2018, in New Jersey, I recall having a memorable, thoughtful discussion with a dozen or so senior leaders in a global corporate. We discussed whether corporate kissing and hugging is a thing of the past. We dissected in detail whether this sort of thing had ever, in fact, been genuinely acceptable and for whom. I think we came out thinking that it was probably a shame if physical contact between work colleagues was now a thing of the past. Sometimes, for some people, it can provide an important support.

At some point in the discussion the question was asked, I think partly in jest, *are we saying I have to get permission before I hug someone?* The answer the group found was that we're human beings, we have highly developed senses; we actually know in the moment, *if we look for it, if we notice*, how the other person is viewing the action we're proposing.

In that split second (in which we offer physical contact to another human being) we can tell whether that contact is welcome. We just need to be more aware of the signals.

It's not about actually asking, *can I have a hug?* Because the person may feel duty bound to accept, particularly if you're their boss. It's about reading the signs. This is a great example of the social sensitivity we talked about in Chapter 3. Post *#MeToo* it seems to me that firms have a choice as regards behaviour: they can introduce detailed behavioural rules or they can rely on the integrity of their people to behave in a befitting manner.

In that discussion in New Jersey, the leaders saw that their challenge was to articulate professionalism. For me, this is about role modelling and allowing integrity to govern everything you do, including the automatic social decisions about human interaction each of us make at work and elsewhere. Because those decisions will impact on other people.

IS INTEGRITY REALLY JUST FOCUSING ON IMPACT?

It's absolutely possible to view integrity simply as an extension of the principle I've expounded in this book, of focusing on impact rather than on intent. The standard dictionary definitions of integrity allow this, particularly the secondary meaning (because the primary meaning doesn't take us much further).

The primary meaning according to Oxford Living Dictionaries is:

> *(1) The quality of being honest and having strong moral principles.*

From the cross-cultural work I've done, I know that the word **honest** is something of a chameleon: it means different things to people brought up in different countries or in different ways. In a task-based culture (such as the US or the UK), whether you're acting honestly will have much to do with doing what you've said you'll do. Whereas, in a relationship-based culture (more prevalent in Asia, Africa or South America), the question of honesty is likely to involve some consideration of allowing yourself and others to save face.

What's more, in any cultural setting the context in which you've been asked a question is important. There are certain softer cultural expectations at play here. When your partner asks you how they look. When your boss asks you how your colleagues are performing. How honest should you be?

Neither is **morality** much clearer. It concerns the distinction between right and wrong and is where the phrase *doing the right thing* as a proxy for integrity comes from. Being right, like being honest, is a far more complicated idea than might at first appear. We've already looked at the idea that there's often more than one rule to consider, and at Camus' suggestion that your personal rules should prevail.

Perhaps to make it simpler, let's focus on the secondary meaning of integrity.[52] It may unwittingly help us:

(2) the status of being whole and undivided.

In order to check that we're acting with integrity, we have to look at **the whole thing**, we have to look through a number of different lenses and weigh up the disparate impacts of our behaviour.

For some years now I've asked groups of people at work to list the people to whom they're accountable, to whom they may have to answer for the way they act at work. It's a fascinating process, watching a group create a list of the sort I set out below. Given five minutes, any group will come up with perhaps 20-plus ideas of the people or groups of people they ought to have in their mind.

My sense is that people intellectually understand that they're accountable; they just don't often think in the moment about the people who may view their day-to-day behaviour.

In the exercise, five constituencies emerge very quickly.

1. **You**: primarily you're accountable to yourself. And to **your people**. This will include your family and the people you represent (your teachers, your friends, perhaps the people running your corner shop, and, possibly, the wider community you live in). Your core beliefs, principles, or purpose will also be important if you have spent time and effort distilling them, as will your deity or religion (if you have one).

2. **External stakeholders**: a stakeholder in this context means anyone who relies on you (anyone who has a stake in how you behave). This will include your clients, customers, and the people you serve. Also shareholders and investors in, and suppliers to, your organisation. It's wider than that though: the rest of your industry are stakeholders too – your competitors and any trade bodies.

   If one footballer, estate agent, social worker, or politician abuses their position, all of them and everyone attached to their industry suffers to some degree.

3. **Internal stakeholders**: everyone in your organisation has a stake in how you behave at work. Starting with the people in your team, those you work with every day, your manager, your manager's manager, other teams, other departments, people you work less often with etc.

Just stopping at this point, it's easy to see that different representatives from each of these three areas will have a slightly different lens, a different expectation of you and how you should perform your task. Your Mum, a client, and Raj or Wendy in accounts will expect slightly different things. As we move on to areas four and five, this changes a little.

4. **Enforcers:** this group will look at workplace behaviour differently. There are two principal types of enforcer.

   a) Internal enforcers: increasingly, larger organisations have specialist functions such as compliance, legal, audit, HR. These specialists will have particular views on how a job should be done and how you should behave with your colleagues.

b) **External enforcers**: in most industries the role of a regulator is obvious and growing. Their rules will often overlap society's laws. Professionally, I've always found this area very interesting. Most people don't think that much about the police, courts, and tribunals as they go about their jobs. Perhaps they should?

I'm reminded of what Tom Hays, the trader described in court as the ringmaster of the LIBOR rigging scandal, and currently serving 11 years in jail, said in his evidence: *Did I think I'd get a medal from the regulator for it, no. Equally I didn't think I was Bernie Madoff.*

At least he had the regulator in his mind! Of course, Hays illustrated how we all tend to prioritise the impact that something may have on ourselves (and possibly those we love) rather than its impact on others. All human beings display an innate desire to rationalise, to explain what we've done from our own perspective. We all tend to see things in a way that suits us.

Integrity is about not seeing things simply in a way that suits us, and not justifying the behaviour from our own perspective. It's about considering the diverse impacts our actions have on everyone who will, potentially, be affected.

Finally (and normally quite late in the discussion) people will start to talk about the final area.

5. **Wider society**: people not directly reliant on you; not stakeholders, but people who are somehow interested. Here we might be talking about the end users of the products you create. We could be talking about future generations not yet born – particularly with decisions that impact upon the environment.

If almost anyone performs their job badly (or to a lesser extent well), people in society will have a view, almost no matter who they are or what job they have. Increasingly they will express that idea on social media. That could then be picked up in what used to be called the mainstream media.

Increasingly we're accountable to everyone. There's a whole other book (probably many books) on that paragraph alone. I'm just focusing now on how we need to use an increased sense of accountability to drive integrity.

INTEGRITY – A STEP-BY-STEP GUIDE!

From analyzing these five constituencies of accountability, a simple framework arises. It'll take you a little time to use, but if you are being more mindful, you'll give yourself more opportunities to think in this way. And you won't have to do it for every action. Only those that may negatively impact on others.

I suggest you start with Box 1, **you and your people**. This is *the* critical bucket, and where you'll probably spend most of your time. If you can get out of here, you're likely to be acting with integrity.

Ask yourself the **first question**:

Am I being true to myself? Is this an honest and right thing for me to do?

If you've identified your purpose, you could add this into the mix too, *am I being true to myself **and my purpose**?* Only if you think you are (and it is), can you proceed.

You'll develop your own sense of what's honest. I've come to see deception as being an important part of my sense of honesty: *has anyone been deceived?* When it comes to whether the thing is right, in this bucket you're using your own rules, your own sense of right.

If you answer the first question in the affirmative, then ask the **second question** about your people:

*Would **they** see this as an honest and right thing for me to do?*

Here you have to put yourself in the minds of your mother, your primary school teacher, or the family running your corner shop etc. You have to imagine explaining to them what you are going to do/are doing/have just done and asking them whether **in their mind** it's an honest and right thing for **you** to do. Remember it's not whether they would do it themselves, it's about their assessment of whether it's something that's honest and right for **you** to do.

If it's clear to you that someone's rules are being broken, the thing you're doing may still be right. However, in that case you'll normally need to have weighed up how many people may benefit and how many may be harmed by what you're doing or planning to do.

If you have enough doubts about the action to engage fully in this process in the first place, then Box 1 will take some getting out of. Always remember too, if you're in any doubt, you can always (in fact, you probably should) have conversations with your people rather than just imagining those conversations. It can be important to get someone else's perspective on any ethical dilemma. It's often the easiest way of working out whether you're acting with integrity.

If you do get out of Box 1, then move to Box 2 (external stakeholders); think about the various people in that box and ask yourself the **second question** (this time about the people in that box):

Would they see it as an honest and right thing for me to do?

When you come to someone who you doubt would see this as an *honest* and *right* thing for you to do, you have to respect and give value to what you think they would believe. Be clear, you're always imagining asking whether it's an honest and right thing for **you** to do. A third party may argue that they will be harmed, but if others will benefit, you may still be acting with integrity if you do it.

You give value to others' views by *imagining the conversation you would have with them; how would you persuade them that this is an honest and right thing for you to do?*

Perhaps you could adapt what you are doing, so they would see this as an honest and right thing for you to do.

As I've said, when you start imagining conversations with enforcers (in Box 4) things might change, the lens that enforcers use is normally very different to yours. I've spent much of my career helping people see that.

JUST HOW BIG ACTUALLY IS INTEGRITY?

As I've grasped more of its meaning I've started to recognise just how important integrity is. I've started to wonder if it might challenge love as being *the* thing that really matters. I don't think it sounds quite as good: *there's only one thing that matters: integrity.* Maybe you disagree. It's also occurred to me that love and integrity could actually be the same thing?

In Chapter 1, I said that the workplace proxies for love – **humanity**, **empathy**, and **respect** – were important because they're actually how you treat someone you love. I put forward the idea that we might extend these ideals to the people we work with *just because we work with them* – in the same way as you (are supposed to) extend love to everyone in your family.

Perhaps extending those principles to other people can also be seen as part of integrity? It would certainly be a way of ensuring that you were considering the impact you have on them. Possibly it's the lawyer in me that finally wants to come out and start working on some definitions; please bear with me.

HUMANITY, RESPECT AND EMPATHY – MEAN …

Humanity is the quality of being humane, kind, and benevolent. In my work, I've always tended to place greater emphasis on the word **kind**. In many of the settings I work, for example investment banking or law firms, kind is a word that has been viewed with suspicion, as being *too* soft. I want to reclaim it for corporate use. A synonym that's often used in these settings, particularly in the policies that set out how everyone should behave, is **consideration**. Having consideration for others and their feelings is perhaps where humanity starts?

Amongst the thoughts I've collected for this book is a short, unfinished quote:

> *Once we find our own humanity and we see the humanity in the other person, then we are going to want them to have …*

I don't know where the quote came from. Perhaps from Jo Berry. I like both the exhortation to (search for and) find our own humanity and also that of others. In other words, once we have seen that we are in fact kind and good, and that the other person is too, what are we going to want that other person (or people) to have? Is it what we have? Or perhaps what they want? Is it fair treatment?

I don't know – it's up to you!

As an aside, working on the Headspace app over the last few months I've learnt a very important tool. I now think about my challenges not simply as my own, but as challenges I share with others. The more I see something that exists in my own mind, the more I can see the same challenge in the minds of the people in the café or on the train with me. This simple idea is (as I was told it would be) like a training in empathy. Empathy, by the way, like inclusion, is not something that we do naturally. It's something we have to learn.

The key has been to focus internally first; to see the challenge I'm facing, to clarify exactly what it is. Then to consider how to rise above the challenge, to be a good person. This is an intrinsic part of being kinder to myself. As I've done that, I've seemingly and naturally become aware that other people are doing exactly the same (seeking to be good and to rise above the same sort of problems I'm facing).

Chris Abani is a Nigerian writer who has been imprisoned three times by his government for his views. In his powerful TED talk *On humanity*, Chris tells stories about the magnified impact of various simple acts of kindness he's witnessed. Before you listen to it, I should warn you that Chris has seen and talks openly about some truly horrible things.

He touches on the South African phrase *Ubuntu* and the philosophy it stems from; that there's no way to be human without other people. For someone to be human, others must reflect their humanity back at them. The problem for Abani (and for me and, I assume, for most of us) is that when he looks at himself, he doesn't see his own humanity; what he sees is his own failings, he sees himself cussing at others in traffic.

Always before, when I've looked inside myself, what I've found has always been negative. It's always reflected the tension I've felt about what I'm doing with my life. How I'm not living up to some greater purpose. I've focused on my emotional outbursts, my weaknesses.

Over the last few months, I've started (very tentatively) to see something more positive, possibly to see more of the beardy guru. Someone with a more limited purpose, but a valid one nonetheless.

I'm someone with a purpose, with a positive intent, who (like everyone else) is trying to overcome some difficult challenges, and who's actually done some quite good stuff.

Once we find our own humanity …
What is it we want the other person to have?

Respect is up there with integrity as a word that we use frequently, but most of us would have difficulty explaining it clearly. If you doubt that, again I'd challenge you to do it now. Write down your definition of respect.

Part of the problem is that the word has a dual meaning; you respect someone you hold in esteem (normally because of what they have done or sometimes just who they are). For example, a phrase I hear regularly at the moment is having respect for the *office* of the President.

The second meaning of respect is that you show regard or consideration for the people around you – just because they are human beings. I always focus on this second limb because it contains real, potentially transformative, power.

I regularly ask people in workplaces to talk about what this sort of respect looks like on a Tuesday afternoon in their workplace, in a meeting room or on a conference call. I hear that it's about being listened to or being included in discussions, feeling valued.

I also often hear that it is *being treated how I would like to be treated*. But the problem with treating people how you would like to be treated is that we're all different. You could (just for example) be a cranky, post-operative, workaholic who believes that working all hours is absolutely normal.

You may have no emotional intelligence, you may even be a sociopath! What makes you the best arbiter of how someone else should be treated? Surely respecting someone is at least trying to work out how *they* would like to be treated.

I've already touched on the meaning of **empathy**: it seems to me that nowadays no-one can define the concept without talking about *someone else's shoes*! I've always said that one day I'm going to be brave enough during a workshop and ideally at the end of a day (when participants' feet are at their sweatiest), to get people actually to put on someone else's shoes, to experience what that feels like.

In November 2016, at the Meaning Conference, I encountered the Empathy Museum; **A mile in my shoes**. I walked around the Brighton Dome wearing other people's shoes and listening through headphones to them telling their story. It was seriously impactful. Hearing a stranger talking about the moment he was sent to prison for six years while you are wearing his shoes can only be described as visceral.

Empathy is the *psychological identification with or vicarious experiencing of the thoughts, feelings or attitudes of another*. It's basically trying to understand what is going on in that other person's mind and, **critically**, not judging it as negative (normally, simply because it's not what you think). Much is written about non-judgemental listening. I am clear of two things: (1) it's far from easy, and (2) it's an important skill to have if we're going to succeed.

Trying to bring all that together, what these workplace proxies for love require us to do, is to be kind to ourselves, to focus on the good inside us, and extend kindness and consideration to the other person – thinking about how *they* would like to be treated and how they may be feeling at the moment.

In my work, I always stress that behaving in this way does **not** mean that we can only be soft on the other person.

Look at the paragraph above, we can give them a negative message, we can tell someone they're performing below expectation, possibly even ask them if they are in the right job, provided we do that in with kindness and consideration. Difficult messages are, after all, delivered in families and to loved ones. Quite often I think.

Is acting in this way also part of integrity?

REAL-TIME INTERVENTION 4

I HAVE ACTUALLY
GROWN A BEARD

The beard is far from impressive, but I keep it as an outward sign of the new, purposeful, more fulfilled, and happier me. I grew it during a two-week family holiday in July 2017.

As I completed the final chapters of the book, I was watching a short video of the American purpose guru, Scott Snook, imploring me to *mine my life experiences* to find my purpose. He used the word *wellspring*. I could feel myself getting annoyed. Why use words like *mine* and *wellspring*? What's wrong with words like analyse and source? Keep it simple, don't try to create a new language.

I'm conscious that I'm too judgemental in many things. I know I've got a thing about people creating a new language to make something seem more complex, possibly to make themselves appear cleverer. This supremely judgemental side of me doesn't sit easily with my claim to being liberal. In that moment, watching the video I wondered whether I'm a liberal for whom it's *my way or not at all*. That felt like a problem.

My way or not at all. That probably describes many of us. And that really is the problem. It's symptomatic of a failure to listen, which I've condemned throughout the book. I'm exhorting people to really listen, non-judgementally and to PNLMs – to people outside their bubble. And what do I do?

So I persevered. Mr Snook told me to look at my early childhood experiences, then he said: *look at the really challenging experiences in your life.* I thought *my cancers* and then I thought: *that's where my purpose comes from isn't it?* I hadn't seen it so clearly before.

I went to bed, but slept fitfully. I was on to something. I got up at 4.00am because I needed to re-read the posts I wrote in 2009 during my first cancer. I focused on just how challenging that time had been, how much I had relied on the support of others. How I'd come out of those experiences with a massive sense of purpose. But that sense remained inchoate and unformed. I'd wanted to do something, but I wasn't at all clear what. I left it unfinished.

That early morning I knew I had to start the book with the most important thing – the knowledge that inside each one of us sits the place where good comes from. I had been shown the place and I had wanted to do something with it. But I hadn't. I hadn't challenged the power of normal or done anything extraordinary. Above all, I hadn't started a daily practice motivated by a desire to change.

I feared that I may have to rewrite the whole book. Maybe I could get away with a good edit. It didn't matter, it was just more work (and I'm a workaholic after all).

Reading those posts and some of the messages I'd received from loved ones in 2009 served another really useful purpose. I said in Chapter 8 that some of us may need help seeing our own strengths. I read from the very first message I published in 2009. I received it on the third morning. It said:

You have a capacity for kindness, clarity, integrity and vision that is extraordinary in my experience.

I'd read those words many times; I thought they were lovely. However, I hadn't seen them as I did now. How they absolutely capture my strengths and set me up for the purpose that I have now chosen. *Strengths* was the missing piece of Andy Bird's: values, passions, strengths.

This was all good, things were crystallizing well. Something was playing on my mind though: the horrible sense that I was a fraud. I'd written a whole book about listening to others yet my reaction to Snook's use of the word *wellspring* showed me to be what I knew I was – a judgemental polarist! My wife had written the morning of my psychiatric assessment: *glass always half empty but you're swift to give upbeat advice to others, as if you know better.*

The feeling sat uncomfortably with me for some time, certainly throughout that whole day. I re-read (and inevitably rewrote) what is now the book's Introduction. And that's when it really hit home. I'd now understood that the place I'd seen had nothing to do with heaven. I now saw that choosing or not choosing to visit the place is about choosing to embrace the goodness in you (or not bothering). And that only by embracing the goodness in you can you start to want it for others.

If we choose not to embrace the humanity in ourselves, then normal presides. We experience all sorts of negative thoughts, we follow our limbic brain's toddler tantrums, we behave like we always do. It's only daily practice (in my case enabled by an app) that allows us to access new spaces in our mind and to notice negative thoughts without becoming them.

If we choose to embrace our humanity *and* we practice something daily, we may be *able to* access the place in our mind holding our values and our purpose? If we've created that place, of course. To be clear, none of this is just going to happen.

MY MINING THREW UP SOMETHING ELSE

Snook had also told me to search my experiences for a story that showed I could listen, a time when I'd changed my view. I knew this was important, it would help with my sense of being a fraud. I alighted on a vague memory, but one in which I knew my view changed. It was from 1984, my first year at college. The time of Thatcher and the miners' strike. My adult self was forming.

I remember miners and miners' wives from South Wales coming to speak to us and friends returning from what we now know as the Battle of Orgreave.[53] I also remember my friend Shamik gently putting me right in the matter of Zola Budd and her planned appearance for Great Britain in the 1984 Olympics.[54]

We had debates on a Sunday night. Some were political, some were fun. I didn't normally take part. However, on the Zola Budd question, I had an opinion: that sport and politics should not mix and I put that across (I'm sure far from eloquently).

Shamik was a second year, he studied PPE;[55] he was bespectacled and oozed intelligence. Importantly, given the subject matter, he was from an Indian family. I can't remember if we'd already started to become friends. However, he was gentle with me and treated me respectfully. He said that my idea was noble, something he too wanted to believe. But reality was far removed from that. Sport and politics are inextricably linked, particularly the Olympics in the early 80s!

He has no recollection of our exchange, but a sense of it came back to me very strongly that early morning. With this, an idea formed. I still see Shamik regularly socially. A close friend, someone I love and who my boys love. It hasn't always been smooth between us. At some point, 20-something years ago, the polarist in me judged him for something he'd done. But we've come through that. He still oozes intelligence; whilst I was writing the book he was the Chief Economist at the Foreign Office.

He's also (I think) the only member of my social circle who supports Brexit. I'd always thought *no doubt his arguments are economic?* Strangely, it wasn't something I'd ever asked him about. I suppose because I've never really engaged with anyone on the subject. Not with anyone outside my bubble at least. I told my mother when she sought advice that it was an emotional issue;

that people could construct arguments either way, but deep down you either felt European or you didn't. I felt, I feel, deeply European.

By now I was about 96% of the way through writing a book about reaching outside your bubble, about affecting change by acting the opposite to how you feel. Yet I hadn't ever had a proper conversation about the geo-political question that caused me the most distress. I'd railed with other passionate remainers about how stupid it all was, I'd dissected how it had happened and whose fault it was.

I'd never addressed the issue itself. So now I challenged myself: on Brexit is it *my way or not at all?* The next morning, I emailed Shamik:

> *This is going to sound very grand, but I've realised that I need to talk to you before I can finish my book.*

We met in a pub and chatted. I explained what the book was about and that I really just wanted to listen to his views. I treated it like any diagnostic interview I do at work. I listened carefully. I concentrated on understanding what Sham had said and occasionally on summarising back to him what I'd understood. I didn't respond or counteract, I didn't react emotionally. My job was simply to listen, respectfully.

He'd clearly had this sort of discussion at work many times, but I think seldom socially. He ran me though his arguments on three grounds: economic, political, and identity. When he had finished I commented that I was possibly surprised that he hadn't led with an emotional argument; he hadn't said *I'm a passionate leaver because ...* Probably because I had asked him to explain to me what lay behind his position.

At this point he helpfully ran me through how he would have argued the opposite, Remain position. That consisted of the geo-political importance of big blocs of influence; the threat of a resurgent Russia; the EU being a global standard setter; that we had all become Europeans and that nothing was broken.

Shamik then said something that I took down word for word:

> It's an emotional question, you're absolutely right,
> but the way discussions are conducted ...
> I expect respect from the other side. Instead I get
> howls of outrage. I understand the Remain argument
> and I can see its strengths. You simply don't get that
> from the other side.

The word respect had come from him. He said that the debate should have been (and should continue to be) conducted as we were conducting it. With people laying aside their allegiances and listening respectfully.

It came down to this: the two of us had respect for each other's position. Shamik, as an economist, had long been Eurosceptic because of things like the Common Agricultural Policy. In the discourse around Brexit he felt that the cost of leaving and the benefits of staying had been greatly exaggerated. Also (and again this is the economist talking) you can't have monetary union without political union, and he feels that no-one is being honest enough about that.

Fundamentally though, I felt it probably came down to the fact that he had never felt European in the way that I have, and that he puts real weight on sovereignty in a way that I don't.

I also heard three things that really made me think:

(1) that Texas was effectively bankrupt in the 80s or 90s (in what was called the Savings and Loan (S&L) crisis). I hadn't ever heard about this because Texas, being in a full political union (the USA), was bailed out. Texas, of course, is far bigger than Greece;

(2) that someone whose judgement I trust and who has been much closer to European decision-making than me is really bothered by the elitism that process engenders; and

(3) that Shamik also genuinely believes that in a time-span of between five and 15 years no-one will notice the difference and we will have negotiated our place on the world stage.

I came away from the meeting far happier. I had put to him some of my emotions: for example, that to me, legislation that's European feels somehow better and more important than that of a single nation state. He said that he could understand that I felt that way. Reflecting on it the day after we'd spoken, it was clear to me that my emotional arguments were just that. What made them more important than Shamik's?

A quote that I wrote down the following morning, after my 15 minute daily practice was:

Our perception defines our experience of anything in life.

My perception of Brexit was suddenly more balanced. Perhaps that will be my experience too. It would have been far more difficult for me to do what I did with Shamik with someone I didn't know or love. But had I extended to that person the respect I extended to him, the process of listening could have worked just the same.

Go on, try it!

POSTSCRIPT

WRAPPING IT ALL UP IN A PAGE (AND A HALF)

IF NOT YOU, WHO? IF NOT NOW, WHEN?

1. Observers are key to positive workplace change: in terms of productivity *and* ethics.
2. You'll observe dozens (hundreds?) of times a day. Everything turns on you shining a light on what's happening and:
   a. caring, understanding that simple things really matter *and* being more proactive;
   b. challenging your normal (and things you may have come to see as normal);
   c. having more of the structured conversations that actually change culture;
   d. telling stories that generate emotion in other people and prompt them to change things.

WHY WOULD YOU DO THAT EXACTLY? WHAT'S IN IT FOR YOU?

3. Your humanity is all that matters. Once you've seen that good comes from inside you, you'll want something different for other people.
4. The soft stuff is actually the hard stuff: emotion drives the numbers (the same way it drives all employment problems). Happy people work harder (and tend not to sue).
5. People who bring their whole self to work, who don't compartmentalise, also protect their firms.
6. Possibly because you've made it part of your purpose?

SO, HELP ME WITH THE HOW!

7. Think impact, think first about how everyone in your shadow is feeling. Be considerate.
8. Forget intent (forget seeing everything in a way that suits you). Leave room for other people's thoughts/ideas.

9. Remember the cycle: **how I'm treated → how I feel → how I behave/perform → how I'm viewed → how I'm treated.** Use it to analyse your behaviour and theirs.

UNLEASH THE POWER OF YOU, CHALLENGE THE POWER OF NORMAL

10. Understand your why, ground yourself in now and act with integrity.

11. Individualise ideas like integrity, properly understand them, be able to explain them (using good stories). [Integrity is thinking about your impact on everyone by the way.]

12. You'll never challenge your normal unless you introduce a daily practice. Take time every day to work on yourself, to overcome your mind's negative spiralling.

13. A purpose *can* stop you sleepwalking if it's simple enough to keep at the front of your mind (and you keep it there with daily practice).

14. Finding the intersection of your values, passions and strengths takes effort, but is worth it.

15. Give it a simple name and keep focusing on the path you've chosen.

ENDNOTES

1. 10 January 2017, Chicago.

2. Bullying and harassment have many legal definitions. At its simplest, bullying involves the use of superior strength or influence to intimidate someone, normally to force them to do something. The Access Hollywood tapes in which Trump talks about what you can do (to women) when you are famous would seem to confirm the point.

3. As at June 2018.

4. I would like to publicly acknowledge here the debt I will always owe to Dame Janet Gaymer, the doyenne of employment law and the woman who told me that she wanted me to focus on my training work and build something with it. For completeness, I should probably recount that on hearing this message (which was exactly what I had wanted her to say) I still recall asking whether this meant that she thought I wasn't a very good lawyer!

5. You will have grasped that I am not talking here about physical love. The employment lawyer in me shouts that that should be kept away from the workplace.

6. August 2017.

7. 2.1 million is the approximate population of Slovenia.

8. 'Why gender equality is good for everyone – men included'.

9. 'Employee Engagement: What's your engagement ratio?' Gallup continue to provide this research every year. I still go back to the first version I read because it demonstrates the points I want to make clearly. And nothing that I have read from Gallup (or elsewhere) has subsequently questioned these compelling findings.

10. 'What Google Learned From its Quest to Build the Perfect Team.' The Work Issue, *The New York Times Magazine*, 25 Feb 2016.

11. re: Work.withgoogle.com, Guide: Understanding team effectiveness.

12. ibid.

13. 'Evidence for a Collective Intelligence Factor in the Performance of Human Groups', Anita Williams Wooley, et al Science 330, 686 (2010); DOI: 10.1126/science. 1193147.

14. One important footnote not mentioned in Duhigg's article was that a third factor that correlated to higher collective intelligence was the proportion of females in the group.

15. For the uninitiated, cancer only has 4 stages.

16. It was the middle one – 'get yourself a life and then put work in there somewhere.'

17. Stonewall campaigns for the equality of lesbian, gay, bisexual and trans people.

18. https://www.youtube.com/watch?v=y1SDV8nxypE

19. I'm very conscious that Geert Hofstede used this phrase as a subtitle for his book *Culture and Organizations: Software of the Mind*.

20. *The Chimp Paradox: the mind management programme for confidence, success and happiness*, Professor Steve Peters.

21. As at today's date of writing, about 11 months after starting, my total time meditated is 114 hours; sessions completed 440; with an average duration of 16 minutes. I've done the 30 session packs: Basics, Managing Anxiety, Coping with Cancer, Self-esteem and Sleep, and a 10 session pack on Anger (twice).

22. Sheryl Sandberg's 2016 Commencement Speech at the University of Berkeley, 14 May 2016 (Transcript available on Fortune.com).

23. On making notes of conversations you have with colleagues, I am absolutely clear that this is a good idea. Not least because, as a lawyer, I took hundreds of people down a path they did not want to go down and that path was made far more difficult by the lack of any contemporaneous documentation. However, the paper you create should be 'good paper'. The simple rule is to imagine that you are writing a note that the person you are writing it about will see. If there is a dispute, they are very likely to see it. Imagining them reading the note up-front ensures that what you write will be objective and measured.

24. Best Alternative to a Negotiated Agreement.

25. Roger Fisher and William Ury of Harvard wrote a seminal work on negotiation: *Getting to yes: Negotiating Agreement without Giving in*.

26. Time to Think: Listening to Ignite the Human Mind.

27. Broockman and Kalla, 'Durably reducing transphobia; a field experiment on door-to-door canvassing'. Science 352, no. 6282 (8 April 2016): pp. 220-224.

28. Gecan's most famous work is *Going Public: an organizer's guide to citizen action* (2002).

29. I have brought elements of two similar situations together to ensure confidentiality is not threatened.

30. I'm indebted to my colleague Eleanor Handley for respectfully pointing out to me that *tell me*, which I insisted for years was my favourite question, is actually a directive not a question!

31. *The Leader's Shadow: Exploring and Developing Executive Character. SAGE*, 6 March 1999.

32. If anyone I'm talking to suggests that shadow (for them) bears some sort of negative connotation probably because they have studied Jung – I say that that's not how I'm using the term at all.

33. Dr Bastian Schiller (Freiburg) and team from the University of Basel, published in Proceedings of the National Academy of Sciences.

34. Kahneman is an Israeli-American psychologist awarded the Nobel Memorial Prize in 2002, who wrote *Thinking Fast and Slow* in 2011.

35. It's important that you understand, by the way, that the other person will probably understand that you are doing that.

36. An international body that monitors and makes recommendations about the global financial system including how to improve market and institutional resilience.

37. 'Inclusive capitalism: creating a sense of the systemic', a speech made by Mark Carney at the Inclusive Capitalism Conference: London, 27 May 2014.

38. Michael Kimmel: *Angry White Men: American Masculinity and the End of an Era* (2013): The Nation Institute

39. Paul Polman interviewed by his son Sebastian on Huffington Post's *Talk to Me*.

40. 'The Age of Consumer Capitalism', *Harvard Business Review*, Jan-Feb 2010 issue.

41. Michael C Jensen and William H Meckling 'Theory of the Firm; Management Behavior, Agency Costs and Ownership Structure' published in the *Journal of Financial Economics 1976*.

42. In support of their thesis Craig quotes HBR research among 20,000 employees that 'employees with a strong sense of purpose' are '76% more satisfied with their jobs, 56% more engaged and 100% more likely to stay with their organisation'.

43. Jason Burnham is the Principal of Experience Innovation Strativity Group, Inc. and his professional purpose is to improve how businesses operate and innovate towards creating a better tomorrow.

44. 13,381,929 views as at 17 February 2019.

45. Jorge is now an Associate Client Partner at Korn Ferry.

46. Honestly, the first word I want to write, because it is always there, in how I think and feel, is cancer. But I want to believe that it has not become part of the essence of me.

47. 'Tinkering: attempt to improve something in a casual or desultory way.' (You would not believe how many times I've gone through drafts of the chapters of this book for example!)

48. I'd discussed these questions with others twice in facilitated workshops, I then sat down for a whole morning and worked hard at it – this is a long, hard slog remember!

49. 1. Who are you? 2. What do you love to do? 3. Who do you do it for? 4. What do those people need? 5. What changes as a result?

50. https://vimeo.com/176370337

51. *MailOnline*, 12 June 2018.

52. Oxford Living Dictionaries.

53. A violent confrontation on 18 June, 1984 between police and pickets at a British Steel Corporation coking plant in Orgreave, South Yorkshire. A pivotal event in the 1984-85 miners' strike.

54. Budd was a young white South African runner sponsored by the Daily Mail who was granted British citizenship in a very short time so that she could compete in the Los Angeles Olympics.

55. Philosophy, Politics and Economics.

AN INTRODUCTION TO
MATT DEAN

Matt has always struggled to balance his personal and work lives. A workaholic and inveterate worrier, he worked as an employment lawyer in the City from 1989 to 2003. Recognised as a truly inspiring facilitator, since 2003 Matt has worked all over the world using straightforward ideas that challenge people to change their bit of the workplace.

Matt's proudest achievement is a (currently 25 year) marriage with life/work partner Victoria Byrne. They live in Sussex with three boys apparently insistent on becoming adults and possibly more animals than Matt would have chosen for himself. Together they co-founded byrne·dean in 2003, a firm dedicated to creating kinder, fairer, more productive workplaces.